PICKING UP
the
PIECES

2/18/23

TO Jim and Sue,
I hope that this book
encourages and blesses
you. I apologize for
the length of time that
it hed tcken to send
it to you.
Jary

PICKING UP
the
PIECES

Forewords by
Dr John Clements and Andy Biddlecombe

JAN TAYLOR

A Biblical perspective for rebuilding our future

Ø **Zaccmedia**

Published by Zaccmedia
www.zaccmedia.com
info@zaccmedia.com

Published October 2020

ISBN: 978-1-911211-97-6

British Library Cataloguing-in-Publication Data.
A catalogue record for this book is available from the British Library.

This book is dedicated to Maybug, Michael, Jill, Phil, Helen, Carl, Carolyn, Joyce, David, Janet, Marie, Tim, Jane, Eddie, Louise, Sally, David, Maureen, and John.

≈

CONTENTS

He is wooing you from the jaws of distress to a spacious place free from restriction, to the comfort of your table laden with choice food.

JOB 36:16; NIV

I will repay you for the years the locusts have eaten, the great locust and the young locust, the other locusts and the locust swarm – my great army that I sent among you.

JOEL 2:25; NIV

FOREWORD BY
DR JOHN CLEMENTS

Are you drenched? No, I am not asking if you have been caught out in a thunderstorm without a raincoat or umbrella. What I am referring to is your life, is it soaked in the Word of God? I am delighted to tell you that as you read this book you will find teaching from the Bible on every page. The one thing that all leading Christians throughout history share is their love of scripture. If you want a victorious and powerful life, then reading books like this will help you on your journey.

This book is more than just a commentary on the Old Testament books of Ezra and Nehemiah, covering a period of Jewish history from around the fall of Jerusalem in 539 BC and ends in the second half of the fifth century. Jan not only skilfully unpacks this history but relates it to our everyday lives. She does this by drawing from insights gained from her own life. But what I really like is her honesty in sharing some painful experiences from her own Christian journey. She unpacks many important aspects of the Christian life from prayer to spiritual warfare, from disobedience to failure, from Christian lifestyle to spiritual revival. The list of topics covered are too long to be given here but she has provided a helpful index where she lists them all. The book is peppered with references from the New Testament, so make sure that you have a copy of your Bible handy so that you can look them up.

The early Puritans were given the name of God Watchers. Nothing encourages our faith more than following the hand of God through the pages of history. I am so pleased that Jan has written about this period in the Old Testament which most people neglect to read yet Jan brings it to life in simple everyday language. Far from being outdated the message of these books is as relevant today as was when they were first written. God has enabled Jan to see how these Old Testament books have a message for us today as we face the current pandemic of the Covid 19 virus. Just like those exiles of long ago we are facing uncertainty, fear and change. Does God have anything to say to us today from His word? Read this little book and you will see how Jan raises some important questions which we should consider. One thing is certain today as it was then, the virus has changed our world just as the exile changed theirs. They needed the walls of Jerusalem to be rebuilt, we need to revival in the Church.

Whilst you can probably read this little book in a matter of a few hours, yet it might take you the next 3-5 years to apply its teaching to your life! I can highly recommend this book to Christians of all ages and I am confident that we all can all benefit from reading it, I know I certainly did and pray that you do the same.

Praying that the Lord will enrich your life.

Dr John Clements

Dr John Clements is pastor of the Old Meeting House Congregational Church, Norwich which was gathered by the Puritan William Bridge in 1643. He is the author of a number of books including *How to Get What Money Can't Buy: Personal Peace and Happiness in a World of Unrest.*

FOREWORD BY ANDY BIDDLECOMBE

There's probably never been a year in any of our lives quite like 2020. The current global pandemic means everyday normality, as we knew it, feels miles away from this moment.

Lockdown, social distancing, quarantine and so on, are rupturing society to its core, with heartbreak and strains that go well beyond our own doorsteps.

Across the country and around the world, many of us have found ourselves crying out to God from new depths of vulnerability and uncertainty. Like exiles in a foreign land, we yearn for the familiarity of the old things, but they're out of reach, crumbling, dismantling, and drifting away, some gone for good.

In 'Picking Up the Pieces' Jan gives us a cause for hope. This book is an inspiring invitation to stop and reflect on the parallels and similarities of our current situation with the epic Biblical story of rebuilding, as told in Ezra and Nehemiah.

Combining Old and New Testament references, as well as drawing from her own life experiences, Jan suggests some important lessons and principles we could adopt for the times we're in; potential keys to faith and wisdom in so many of the realities we're facing right now.

With an emphasis on restoration and kingdom principles, her accessible study notes could be a timely guide as we each come to terms with the places we find ourselves both spiritually and relationally.

So many of us who have a passion for healing ministries, and for building church and community, are currently facing all kinds of questions, individually and together, as we seek to gain discernment and a grasp of what God is saying to us in this unanticipated moment.

Jan reminds us that this liminal space can be welcomed as an opportunity and a gift, if we give time and space to seek God and go deeper in Him and with each other, and commit, not to paper over cracks and issues that are being brought to light. Some wounds, some reconciliations, take a longer time to heal and turn around than we'd like, but there's wisdom in the waiting.

The Biblical principles, to which Jan points, remind us to renew our commitment to the overall commission and really focus. To truly care about rebuilding and maintenance of lives and relationships. And, through all the ups and downs of sadness and celebrations, endings and new beginnings, to embrace stronger foundations and clearer vision.

After all, we haven't arrived here simply to return to how things always were! Whatever our new normal might look like, we need to discover it with God's guidance, not just through government guidelines. The message of the book is that this is not a comfortable place to be, but it could be a healthy one.

Andy Biddlecombe
– Founder and co-leader of Wildfire

INTRODUCTION

I am writing this book in the middle of the pandemic, and I am conscious that people all over the world have been and are crying out to God for deliverance from it. Not only that, but there are also a great number of people who are trying to work out why it has happened and coming up with a variety of different theories, some rather more far-fetched than others! However, God is the only one who knows for sure the cause of the virus, and I have to admit that I am not sure we need to know what that is at this point, if at all, as there are undoubtedly far more crucial questions to be answered than the reason.

In fact, I think the most important thing for us to recognise now is that what we are currently experiencing would not be happening if God had not allowed it. From my perspective, it means the most important question we need to ask for now is why He has done so. Since I am confident that there is more than one answer to that question, I am not going to share my thoughts about it now. Having said that, some of them will become apparent in what I say in this book.

However, our answer to this question will indicate what action we need to take and perhaps give us some direction for our lives. Also, we need to recognise that until the purpose has been fulfilled, things are not going to become whatever normal is going to look like in the future. I am saying this because I am sure our lives are never going to be the same again. The reason that I say that is because I am certain that things are never going to be the same again, so it is important for us all to recognise this. For us to able to rebuild our lives and our communities we will need to work in partnership with God because we will need His wisdom and counsel in order to be able to do it well.

What may perhaps be of interest to you is that I had started to write another book, but shortly after the lockdown came, I felt God was prompting me to put that one aside for the time being so that I could write this one. My goal in writing this book is to look at and discuss some of the biblical principles that will enable us to rebuild our lives and restore our church communities after the pandemic is over. Such principles will undoubtedly have a wider application as well as being invaluable whenever something happens that either damage our communities or us.

This book is based on two Old Testament books, Ezra and Nehemiah, which from my perspective, resonate with our situation and therefore have much to teach us. The reason I believe this is because they speak about the rebuilding and restoration of the people of Jerusalem, their city and the Temple, their place of worship, after a war, and in a sense, we are in a similar situation. As was the case with my previous book, *The Esther Strategy*, I will be writing about some of the history spoken of in both books, but will keep it to the minimum because I know that not everyone enjoys it in the way I do!

You may find it helpful to know that at this point, Ezra

and Nehemiah themselves speak of events at the end of the Babylonian Empire and the beginning of the Persian one, i.e., between the late sixth and early fifth century BC. Moreover, the two books were originally one but were separated in the Latin Christian tradition of the late medieval era. The Books of Ezra and Nehemiah were both written by Ezra, a scribe who was living in Babylon at the beginning of the book that was named after himself. Furthermore, it is generally thought that he also wrote 1 and 2 Chronicles.

As always, my starting point in writing this book is the Bible, which for me is the plumb line of truth;[1] everything I say flows out of it. I also recognise that how I interpret things may not fit with your understanding of them. I am conscious too that none of us has a monopoly on the truth, so if you feel I have said something not helpful to you in your journey into God's heart, feel free to discard it.

If you have read any of my other books, you may notice one or two differences in how I have done things this time, which I hope you will enjoy. Also, I have put in a timeline and an index of keywords/themes. Should you want to give me some feedback in any way, my email address is at the back of the book as usual.

Jan Taylor
June 2020

---

1 1 Timothy 3:16-17; Hebrews 4:12

TIMELINE

JERUSALEM

Zerubbabel, Sheshbazaar return 538BC

Rebuilding the Temple began 537 BC

Temple building started again in 520BC and finished in 516 BC

Ezra arrives 438 BC

Nehemiah governor from 445-433 BC

KINGS OF THE PERSIAN EMPIRE

Cyrus 538-530 BC

Cambyses 530-520 BC

Darius 522-486 BC

Xerxes 486-485 BC

Artaxerxes 464-423 BC

1

NEW BEGINNINGS

In the first year of Cyrus king of Persia, in order to fulfil the word of the Lord spoken by Jeremiah, the Lord moved the heart of Cyrus king of Persia to make a proclamation throughout his realm and also to put it in writing: This is what Cyrus king of Persia says: The Lord, the God of heaven, has given me all the kingdoms of the earth and he has appointed me to build a temple for him at Jerusalem in Judah.

(Ezra 1:1-2; NIV)

Before we look at the above quotation, we need to briefly talk about the history that led up to what is spoken about. This is because if we ignore it, we will not have sufficient understanding of the background to be able to put it in context. Let me begin by saying that both Israel and Judah had been invaded several times with devastating consequences before Cyrus became King in about 538 BC. Each invasion had resulted in not just many deaths, but in large numbers of people being sent into exile. The Bible clearly links these events to their disobedience to God. In fact, those of you who know your Bible well will be aware that there were numerous prophetic warnings given to them about continuing in their disobedient lifestyle.[2]

The involvement of Cyrus the Great in rebuilding the Temple in Jerusalem was prophesied by Isaiah many years before he became king.[3] This tells us that God chose him for that very purpose. That is an interesting thought to ponder as it raises all sorts of questions, particularly about the issue of predestination. Moreover, it is unlikely that Cyrus would have been seen by the believers of his day as necessarily being the most likely candidate for the task—unless of course, they were aware of the prophecies about him which were mentioned earlier.

Not only that, but it is also a reminder to us all that God often uses those who have little or no significance in the eyes of those around them, to do the kind of things that no one would have expected them to even do, let alone achieve.[4] Whilst there are numerous examples of such people throughout the Bible, it is not possible to read the gospels without finding plenty of people who would have fallen into this category, one notable one being the woman at the well.[5]

However, one of my favourite stories of this ilk is that of Ruth. Her story is an amazing one; she was a Moabitess who was part of Mary's bloodline[6] and is, therefore, part of Jesus' too. If you have never read the book that contains her story,

---

2   For example: Jeremiah 14:1-10; 21:1-14
3   See Isaiah 44:24-28; 45:13
4   1 Corinthian 1:26-29
5   John 4:1-26; 39-42
6   Matthew 1:1-16

I encourage you to do so as it will build faith in you for your future.

Returning to the proclamation, we now read:

Any of his people among you may go up to Jerusalem in Judah and build the temple of the Lord, the God of Israel, the God who is in Jerusalem, and may their God be with them. And in locality where survivors may now be living the people are to provide them with silver and gold, with goods and livestock, and with freewill offerings for the temple of God in Jerusalem. (Ezra 1:3-4; NIV)

In this part of the announcement, we see that Cyrus gave his permission to anyone who had been exiled from Judah who wanted to return home to do so,[7] which was clearly a fulfilment of God's promise to His people. In fact, from this one event, we catch a glimpse of something of God's character and nature because of the way that He kept His Word. It speaks about His faithfulness and kindness towards the Jewish people even after they have not been particularly faithful to Him. Also, it serves as a reminder of the amazing grace of God towards every one of us.

What is also astounding about this proclamation is how those around the exiles, many of whom would not have been Jewish, were encouraged to support those who wanted to return home in various ways. Ezra goes on to record the way in which the people responded to the proclamation:

All their neighbours assisted them with articles of silver and gold, with goods and livestock, and with valuable gifts, in addition to all the freewill offerings. (Ezra 1:6)

---

7   Jeremiah 29:10-14

It is worth noting that in this verse, we see the first of several allusions to the Exodus.[8] This would have indicated to all those who were Jewish who read it to see what was happening as a deliverance just as that had been. But for us Christians, the exodus from Egypt, the land of slavery, is a picture of our journey out of the bondage of sin.[9] Moreover, the Promised Land that God gave to the Jewish people is the equivalent of the fulfilment of God's purposes for us as individuals as well as His eternal purpose for us corporately as the Bride of Christ.[10]

It is perhaps worth noting at this point that what is often referred to as being the story of salvation is not just about getting our sin dealt with or a ticket to heaven; there is far more to it than that. *Sozo*, one of the Greek words, often translated as speaking about salvation, can also be translated as healed[11] and made well. In other words, it means more than just being saved.[12] Since healing can be defined as the putting of a life into divine order, salvation is best described as a journey into wholeness and restoration.

Now, regarding what Cyrus did for the exiles, it did not finish with the proclamation as he went on to return the articles that had been seized from the Temple in Jerusalem many years earlier by the king of that time, Nebuchadnezzar. They were given to the then-current prince of Judah, Sheshbazzar, to transport back to Jerusalem when he returned there.[13] In this too are allusions to the exodus, which is something of a motif through both Ezra and Nehemiah. In fact, Isaiah 52:11-12 makes it clear that the

---

8   Exodus 3:18-22; 11:1-3; 12:33-36
9   Colossians 2:6-15
10   Revelation 19:6-9
11   Mark 10:46-52; John 42b-48
12   John 10:9; Romans 5:9
13   Ezra 1:7-11

return of these vessels was part of what would be involved in a 'second exodus.' However, there is another, and perhaps a more important point that needs to be made about the return of these items. The key to this can be found in the verse just after the last one quoted:

Moreover, King Cyrus brought out the articles belonging to the temple of the Lord, which Nebuchadnezzar had carried away from Jerusalem and placed in the temple of his God. (Ezra 1:7; NIV)

This is the second time in the first seven verses of the book that these vessels are spoken of. This is not primarily because of their value but because of something that is of greater worth. The return of these vessels would have been a picture for all those returning to Judah to rebuild the Temple in Jerusalem for a strong line of continuity with regard to the central role it had played in their lives before the exile. Besides, their return would undoubtedly have helped to build and solidify the unity of all those who were going back to their homes.[14] This would have been the case because it would have reminded them of all the sacrifices, rituals, feasts, etc., that they had shared together previously. Furthermore, as most, if not all of us, know such shared experiences create bonds that tie people together.

Whilst as Christians we do not need a specific place to worship God, we are called to meet together[15] since we:

...like living stones are being built into a spiritual house to be

---

14   Ezra 1:8-11
15   Hebrews 10:25

a holy priesthood, offering spiritual sacrifices acceptable to God
through Jesus Christ.   (1 Peter 4:4; NIV)

Moreover, our unity is not based on a geographical location
but on our relationship with God and the understanding of
His Word. To put it another way, our unity flows out of what we
have in common, rather than on traditions, sacrifices, rituals,
or even feasts. Also, in Ephesians 4:3, we are encouraged to:

Make every effort to keep the unity of the Spirit through the bond
of peace.

For us, therefore, one of the biggest keys to our unity lies in
how well we relate to one another. In other words, we cannot
just sweep our difficulties with each other under the carpet
and pretend that they do not exist. This is because doing so
will not restore peace and will ultimately affect our unity as
a body.

Perhaps we need to remind each other and ourselves from
time to time that we are encouraged at various points in the
New Testament, to work through the issues we have with one
another. In fact, Jesus gave us a process for doing so. If you do
not know the Bible well and are not aware of what is involved
in that process, it is described in Matthew 18:15-17. However,
when you use it, remember that the method described is meant
be done in love[16] and is not about making the offending party
pay heavily for their wrongdoing, even though the making of
restitution may prove to be a necessary part of the process.[17]

---

16   Ephesians 4:32; 1 Timothy 5:1-2; 2 Timothy 4:2
17   Numbers 5:5-7

We must not forget that God's heart for us is to be reconciled to one another if possible. He is after all the God who heals and restores, as evident in the parable of the Lost Son in Luke 15:11-24. Moreover, since our journey into His heart for us involves incarnating Christ so that we increasingly become more like Him,[18] seeking to be reconciled with people we have hurt, and those who have wounded us should be something that we actively work towards.

I will never forget being in what was a rather large church meeting some years ago in which an incredible reconciliation took place between a father and a son. The father was visiting the area and happened to be in that meeting. He had been alienated from his son for some years and did not even realise that he was visiting the church that his son was now part of. What happened that day was that we had a visiting speaker who brought a prophetic word for the son that spoke into his relationship with his father in detail. The son was asked to stand in response to the word, and the father saw him. As a result, they were reunited, and their relationship was restored.

Ezra records that more than fifty thousand people returned to Judah at this point in the story,[19] and the historical records available at present tell us that this happened in about 538 BC. When they returned to Judah, they initially gathered in Jerusalem[20] before returning to their hometowns.[21] A while later, they gathered again to start the work they had returned home to do.[22]

---

18   2 Corinthians 3:18
19   Ezra 2:1-67
20   Ezra 2:68-69
21   Ezra 2:70
22   Ezra 3:1

Let me finish this chapter by saying that Ezra gives us quite a lot of details about the exiles who returned to Judah which may seem to be superfluous, and perhaps even unnecessary, in terms of the story. However, it is more than possible that such details have been included to show us something about the heart of God, not just for individuals, but also for families.

2

REBUILDING THE ALTAR

When the seventh month came, and the Israelites had settled
in their towns, the people assembled together as one in
Jerusalem. Then Joshua son of Jozadak and his fellow priests
and Zerubbabel son of Shealtiel and his associates began to
build the altar of the God of Israel to sacrifice burnt offerings
on it, in accordance with what is written in the law of Moses
the man of God.

(Ezra 3:1-2; NIV)

When the people gathered to start the work of rebuilding the Temple, the first thing they did was to rebuild the altar so that the regular sacrifices required by the Law could be made once again. For the people of God of that time, worshipping God involved not just the making of sacrifices but also obedience to numerous commandments—along with a multitude of rituals and feasts. Their pattern of worship flowed out of the many commandments that form part of what is now referred to as being the Old Covenant.

This, of course, contrasts sharply in many ways with what worship means for us as Christians. Worshipping God, at its core, is about love[23] and living a surrendered life[24] in partnership with the Holy Spirit.[25] However, this does not mean that the Old Testament has is nothing to teach us, because it is incredibly rich in spiritual truth. As such, we can learn a lot about the nature and character of God as well as about the principles of what some refer to as being Kingdom living.

In the Old Testament era, altars and places of worship were generally seen as being about physical locations. But for us, it is primarily about lifestyle and our hearts. This is because true worship [26]is not just about our words, but also concerns our thoughts, motives, and actions. Jesus said,

> *"...What comes out of a person is what defiles them. For it is from within, out of a person's heart, that evil thoughts come – sexual immorality, theft, murder. Adultery, greed, malice, lewdness, envy, slander, arrogance and folly. All these evils come from inside and defile a person."*

(Mark 7:20-23)

Such things are what the Bible calls sin. Thankfully, because of Jesus,[27] forgiveness and cleansing are freely available to us,[28] and all we need to do is to ask. Once we have done so, we are then in a place where the Holy Spirit can work with us to bring

---

23   1 John 4:7-13
24   Romans 12:1
25   John 14:15; 26; 16:13
26   John 4:23-24
27   Romans 5:6-10
28   1 John 1:8-9

the necessary repentance and transformation into our hearts and lives.[29]

Returning to the story, we now read that:

Despite their fear of the peoples around them, they built an altar on its foundation and sacrificed burnt offerings on it to the Lord, both the morning and evening sacrifices. Then in accordance with what is written they celebrated the festival of Tabernacles with the required number of burnt offerings prescribed for each day.

(Ezra 3:3-4; NIV)

The way the people of Judah set about rebuilding the altar is particularly noteworthy because those who had returned from exile had been through a time of great difficulty that had separated them from their families and community before doing so. This parallels what we are experiencing in some ways, which is what makes it worth more than just a cursory look.

We now live in a time of history that is unlike any other period we have lived through. So many people are terrified, thinking they might get the virus from someone they encounter in their day-to-day life. While the fear in the quotation was not about a virus, it seems probable in the light of the obvious parallels of this story that we should imitate what the returning exiles did in rebuilding the altar by seeking to ensure that our lives are right before God. Certainly, we need to be asking God to speak to us about our lives, reflecting on what has been and is—perhaps even praying into what is yet to come.

The fact that the first celebrated feast by the former exiles was Tabernacles is also particularly noteworthy because it speaks

---

29   2 Corinthians 3:18

of God being with us. The following quotation speaks into the meaning and significance of this feast, giving us an insight into one of the things God will undoubtedly do in our lives during this time, in preparation for the next season:

Jesus is the ultimate tabernacle or dwelling place of God in human flesh (see John 1:14; Colossians 2:19). *God dwells in our midst through Jesus, who gives us His Spirit in our hearts* (Matthew 18:20). *Jesus will fulfil the feast of Tabernacles at His second coming. There will be a literal rest for the earth and all of its inhabitants. Until then we can know rest in our souls.* [30]

The rest spoken of in the above quotation is sometimes referred to as the rest of faith.[31] This speaks of an unshakeable assurance that God is in control of our lives, and we are not striving or struggling to make our way through life. More than that, we are at peace whether we are living in a season of relative comfort and ease or going through a personal earthquake or storm of some kind. Reaching this *rest* is not generally an automatic thing but something that requires the progressive surrendering of our lives.[32] As such, our ability to rest in God despite what is going on in our lives becomes more evident as we mature in our faith and develop a partnership with the Holy Spirit.

When I first became a Christian in 1986, virtually every difficulty that I went through knocked me sideways. This meant that I was always running to people for support. Over the years, God has done a significant amount of healing and restoration in my life, so my first port of call is usually Him rather than people. I am now much more able to able to rest in Him in

---

30   Page 140 Chapter 8, Celebrating Jesus in the Biblical Feasts
        Dr R Booker, Destiny Image 2016
31   Hebrews 4:1-11
32   Romans 12:1

such times. This does not mean, however, that I no longer look for human support, but it means I do not generally ask for help now unless I need it.

Just as God's people of the day saw the need to establish a rhythm or pattern of daily worship so perhaps should we:

> *After that, they presented the regular burnt offerings, the New Moon sacrifices and the sacrifices for all the appointed sacred festivals of the Lord, as well as those brought as freewill offerings to the Lord.*
>
> (Ezra 3:5; NIV)

While our pattern will not look anything like theirs, primarily because of the difference in the way we worship, we can nevertheless establish our own by having regular devotional times, etc. Living a lifestyle of worship does not mean such things are precluded because, after all, if we are not regularly spending time with God and reading His Word, then our relationship with Him will not grow—neither can we mature in our faith.

> *On the first day of the seventh month they began to offer burnt offerings to the Lord, even though the foundation of the Lord's Temple had not yet been laid.*
>
> (Ezra 3:6; NIV)

What this verse makes it plain is that the people of Judah did not wait until the circumstances were better to establish a rhythm of daily worship but started from where they were. Whilst what is happening in our lives may not be pleasant, particularly for those who are on furlough or unemployed, it should not stop any of us from re-establishing or creating a pattern of worship in our daily lives.

In doing so, it is vital to think about what our lives may look like after the pandemic finishes, as it may prove much more difficult to continue the rhythm we started with then. If, for example, we are going to be working from nine to five, Monday to Friday, then spending time with God regularly at lunchtime may become difficult to do. Hence, the need to carefully consider the best time for doing so now.

At the early stage of my Christian life, my devotional times were very ad hoc, which resulted in them being infrequent, but in more recent years, I have established a pattern of spending time with God as soon as I have made my first cup of tea of the day. I have found that doing so somehow makes the day not just easier but also run more smoothly. Incidentally, this does not mean that I do not spend any further time with God during the day; the morning devotional time forms the foundation of my daily worship pattern, and I build on it as I feel the need to do so.

While we have been talking about having a pattern for worship, it is perhaps worth reminding ourselves that having a routine is essential to our well-being. If we live in a chaotic way now, it will undoubtedly have a long-term impact on our mental health, so we need to examine how we are using our time. Even if we are not involved in paid employment, it is crucial for us to do some work regularly, whether that is cleaning, gardening, or something else. It is equally essential for us to do some exercise and be involved in a variety of what are best referred to as leisure activities.

Returning to the story we now read:

Then they gave money to the masons and carpenters, and gave food and olive oil to the people of Sidon and Tyre so that they would bring cedar logs by sea from Lebanon to Joppa, as author-ised by Cyrus king of Persia.

(Ezra 3:3-7; NIV)

From this, we can see that before the Temple was rebuilt, a lot of planning was done, including calculating the resources needed for the completion of the work. To put it another way, they set a goal of rebuilding the Temple and then worked towards it. If we do not have goals of some kind, then we will not have any sense of purpose for our lives and will end up living what can only be described as a chaotic existence. Vision does not just give us purpose, but also provides us with hope and results in personal growth.

It is also evident that if the vision for our lives, ministries or churches are truly God-given, then just as King Cyrus provided for the Temple, He will make available to us the resources that we need when we need them. This is because Cyrus is a picture and a type of Christ.

However, this does not mean we will not face opposition or delays of some kind in the fulfilment of that vision. Nor does it mean we will not need to pray for the fulfilment and birthing of the vision. The lockdown might as well be a time God has purposed for you to be able to pray into whatever vision He has already given you. It might also be a period to seek Him for the vision He has for your life, etc., if you do not already have one. Seeing it this way may also help you to turn what could be a negative into a positive, which will undoubtedly have a far-reaching impact in terms of your future.

3

OPPOSITION AND DEFEAT

'In the second month of the second year after their arrival at
the house of God, Zerubbabel son of Shealtiel, Joshua son of
Jozadak and the rest of the people (the priests and the Lev-
ites and all who had returned from the captivity to Jerusalem)
began the work. They appointed Levites twenty years old and
older to supervise the building of the house of the Lord.
(Ezra 3:8-9; NIV)

I t was twenty months after their return from exile that the
Israelites began the work they purposed to do in Judah.
Were they perhaps waiting for the needed materials before
starting? What were they doing with their time during those
twenty months? These are the kind of questions the above
verses generate. However, the Bible does not give us the answer
to those questions. It may be that they used that time to work
on their properties and re-establish relationships, like we have
been doing in this season.

The situation that we are in has given many of us plenty of time to fill, and it is essential for us not to waste it. Instead, we need to use it prayerfully and positively so that we will be prepared for all that God has purposed and promised us regarding our future.

Going back to the story, we now read that:

When the builders laid the foundation of the temple of the Lord, the priests in their vestments and with trumpets, and the Levites (the sons of Asaph) with cymbals, took their places to praise the Lord, as prescribed by David.

(Ezra 3:10; NIV)

Reading about the laying of the foundation of the Temple raises the question of what we see as being the foundation of our faith: Is it the Bible or something else? Our attitude to the Bible is crucial: If we see it as being the plumb line of truth[33] that will have a major impact on our growth and maturity as a believer. This is because only the Word of God gives us a solid foundation on which to build our lives.[34]

The celebration mentioned in this verse must have been an incredible one! Whilst some of the people grieved because they remembered the glory of the previous Temple, the shouts of joy from the rest were so loud that they were, in fact, heard by their enemies.[35] People respond to things in different ways, and we need to remember this in our current season. If we forget, we may find ourselves judging people[36] wrongly for their response

---

33   2 Timothy 3:16-17; Hebrews 4:12
34   Psalm 119:9
35   Ezra 3:11-4:1-3
36   Luke 6:37-38

to what is happening, rather than recognising that God has made us all differently.

Further on in the story we are told how the surrounding peoples reacted to the rebuilding:

'Then the peoples around them set out to discourage the people of Judah and make them afraid to go on building. They bribed officials to work against them and frustrate their plans during the entire reign of Cyrus king of Persia and down to the reign of Darius king of Persia.

(Ezra 4:40-5; NIV)

What a battle the people of Judah faced to rebuild their place of worship and yet they were doing what God wanted them to do! One of the things I have discovered over the years is that whenever we are pressing into God and heading in the right direction, we will almost certainlyly face opposition. This is particularly true of moments or times of significance in terms of His purposes for our lives. However, as Christians, we need to remember that people are not our enemies[37] and:

...our struggle is not against flesh and blood, but against flesh and blood, but against the rulers, against the authorities, against the powers of this dark world and against the spiritual forces of evil in the heavenly realms. (Ephesians 6:12; NIV)

The opposition that we saw in the last quotation from Ezra is just the beginning of the difficulties that were faced by the people of Judah because of their desire to rebuild the Temple

---

37   Matthew 5:43-48

as we will see shortly. The more we desire to do what God wants, rather than living for ourselves, the greater the opposition we will face. However, this is more than compensated for by the increasing sweetness and blessing that will come into our hearts and lives every time we win a battle! The primary keys to winning the battles we are facing, or we will eventually face, lie in ensuring these things:

- We are in a right relationship with God,[38]
- We have put on the armour of God,[39]
- We are using the appropriate kind of weapons,[40]
- And we are working in partnership with the Holy Spirit.[41]

Going back to the story we now are told about further opposition:

At the beginning of the reign of Xerxes, they lodged an accusation against the people of Judah and Jerusalem. And in the reign of Artaxerxes king of Persia, Bishlam, Mithredath, Tabeel and the rest of their associates wrote a letter to Artaxerxes.

(Ezra 4:6-7A; NIV)

Ezra does not give us any further information about the accusation spoken of, although the letter to Artaxerxes is given in full. That letter is full of half-truths and lies,[42] but that is typical of the work of the enemy, who is often referred to as being the father of lies.[43]

---

38   1 John 1:8-10
39   Ephesians 6:13-17
40   2 Corinthians 10:3-4
41   John 16:13
42   Ezra 4:8-16
43   John 8:39-46 note particularly v44

Without being specific there was an occasion some years ago where I was accused of doing something to another woman by another individual. Thankfully, the 'injured party' believed what they were told by someone else, and I was given the benefit of the doubt. Later, however, evidence emerged which completely vindicated me and proved that the person who had made the accusation was, in fact, the guilty party.

To defeat the opposition that we will inevitably face on our journey into God's heart for us, one of the things we need to do is to replace the lies of the enemy with the truth of God's Word. However, we must recognise that finding the right strategy for whatever situation we are facing will involve working in partnership with the Holy Spirit. This is because we will need His intervention to enable us to achieve the breakthrough we are seeking. We may also need people who are willing to hold up our hands just as Aaron and Hur did for Moses,[44] either in prayer or some practical way, or perhaps even both.

King Artaxerxes told Rehum, Shishai, and their associates to stop the work on the Temple after receiving the letter spoken of earlier:

> *...the work on the house of the Lord came to a standstill until the second year of the reign of Darius king of Persia.*

(Ezra 4:24)

Looking at the dates involved, it appears as if the work on the Temple stopped for about eighteen years. At that point, Haggai and Zechariah started prophesying to the people of Judah in

---

44   Exodus 17:8-13

Jerusalem. Their words[45] triggered off the restarting of the work on the Temple. This show us that when God speaks into a situation or life, it is transformed in such a way that what has been said is fulfilled.[46] There are instances like this through the Bible, and one notable New Testament example can be found in Matthew 8:5-13.

Let me also illustrate the point I have just made with a story from my own life. Some years ago, I met up with two of my girlfriends to celebrate my birthday, which happens to be exactly two weeks before Christmas. At the end of our time together, we spent a few moments praying for each other. One of my friends was having trouble conceiving, so I prayed for her to have a Christmas present for the next Christmas holiday. Her son was born just before Christmas the following year, so I believe that I unknowingly prayed out what was already in God's heart for her.

Once again, the work on the Temple was headed up by Zerubbabel, son of Shealtiel and Jeshua son of Jozadak.[47] Tattenai, the Governor of that area, became aware of what was happening and questioned the people involved about their authority to do so. Not entirely satisfied with the answers he was given, Tattenai wrote to King Darius about the situation, but this time, the work on the Temple was allowed to continue. The result was a decree which confirmed what Tattenai had been told as well regarding releasing much-needed resources to those working on the Temple.[48]

We are then told that:

---

45   Haggai 1-23, Zechariah 1:1-8:23
46   Isaiah 55:10-11
47   Ezra 5:1-2
48   Ezra 5:3-5:14

The temple was completed on the third day of the month of Adar, in the sixth year of the reign of King Darius. Then the people of Israel – the priests, the Levites, and the exiles – celebrated the dedication of the house of the Lord with joy.

(Ezekiel 4:15-16; NIV)

What a sense of relief it must have been for the people of Judah when the Temple was finally completed! After such a long-drawn-out struggle to finish it, they must have experienced such a profound sense of release. Their celebrations must have been full of joy, so it is more likely what is said is an understatement.

Both celebration and lament are both spoken of in the Bible, in a manner which indicates that both are seen to be a normal part of our faith journey, yet neither seems to be fully recognised by some Christians in this way. Perhaps we need to look at the nature of the season we are in as individuals and ask ourselves whether, either or even both, are appropriate for us in this time?[49]

As part of their celebrations, the people of Judah made numerous animal sacrifices and installed the priests as required by the law of Moses.[50] Although we are not required to make the kind of sacrifices the people of Judah did, we are called to live sacrificially for God[51] rather than living to please ourselves or others. This is the cost of following Jesus, as can be seen from the verse that follows:

...whoever does not carry their cross and follow me cannot be my disciple.
(Luke 14:27)

---

49   Ecclesiastes 3:1-8 note v4
50   Ezra 6:17-18
51   Romans 12:1; Philippians 2:5-11

However, we all need to recognise that doing so involves a progressive surrendering of our lives.[52] Moreover, that will not be completed until after we have been promoted to glory. If we fail to recognise these things we will constantly struggle with feelings of failure and guilt as we will not always manage to live in the way described.

It is perhaps worth noting that the first feast celebrated after the dedication of the Temple was Passover,[53] which of course is the feast most associated with the Exodus.[54] Not only that, but it also provides us with a picture of the story of our salvation as the Passover lamb is a picture of Jesus.[55]

---

52   Romans 12:1
53   Exodus 12:1-20
54   Ezra 6:19-22
55   Revelation 5:6-10

4

GATHERING AND GROWING

After all these things, during the reign of Artaxerxes king of Persia, Ezra son of Seraiah… came up from Babylon. He was a teacher well versed in the Law of Moses, which the Lord, the God of Israel had given. The king had granted him everything he asked, for the hand of the Lord was upon him. Some of the Israelites … also came up with him to Jerusalem in the seventh year of king Artaxerxes.

(Ezra 7:1-7; NIV)

E zra gives quite an in-depth genealogy for himself that may not mean much to us but would have told the people reading it in his time all they needed to know about his family background. This is because the genealogy given by Ezra clearly shows us that he was descended from Seraiah, one of the last High Priests of pre-exilic Judah, so he was part of the priestly family.

Ezra then went on to tell his readers that he was '*well versed in the law of Moses,*' which for us today would probably be the equivalent of having a Doctorate in Theology. To put it another way, what Ezra did was to establish the basis of his authority to write the books that he wrote for the benefit of his readers.

What particularly stands out in the passage we are discussing is the level of favour he had with King Artaxerxes as he gave him '*everything he asked.*' Studying the lives of others who enjoyed favour of this magnitude seems to suggest that Ezra must have enjoyed a strong relationship with God. However, we need to recognise that none of them sought God for His favour as such; it flowed out of their relationship with Him.

It is worth noting at this point that when Ezra went to Jerusalem, which was probably in about 458 BC, he was accompanied by other exiles who wanted to return to Judah at that time.[56]

Ezra arrived in Jerusalem in the fifth month of the seventh year of the king. He had begun his journey from Babylon on the first day of the first month and he arrived in Jerusalem on the first day of the fifth month, for the gracious hand of his God was upon him For Ezra had devoted himself to the study and observance of the law of the Lord, and to teaching its decrees and laws in Israel.

(Ezra 7:8-10; NIV)

Reading what is said about Ezra's journey to Jerusalem seems to suggest that it did not take as long as perhaps it could have done. However, the fact that the journey took about four months from a modern perspective appears to be an extremely long

---

56   See Ezra 8:1-36 for further details

time, particularly when a flight between the two places would not even take a morning!

As Christians, our lives are about a journey, one which will take us into God's heart and involve the fulfilment of His promises to us. Not only that, when we reach the end of the journey, we will graduate to our eternal home—heaven.[57] Knowing this should instil something of hope and faith needed to keep us going on our earthly pilgrimage.[58]

We are later told that before Ezra left Babylon, King Artaxerxes gave him a letter [59]that commissioned him to:

- invite all those who wanted to return to Judah to come with him,

- take various gifts that had been dedicated to the Temple with him,

- provide certain supplies for the Temple services from the royal treasury when needed, and to,

- appoint people to administer justice in Judah according to the Law of Moses.

Just as the king commissioned Ezra, so we too have been commissioned by Christ. However, whereas his commission was based on a letter, ours is based on living according to what are sometimes referred to as the principles of the Kingdom. Alternatively, another way of looking at it would be living lives that fully reflect what is often referred to as the Great Commission.[60]

Having already been made aware of the completion of the

---

57   1 Peter 2:11; Philippians 3:20-21
58   Psalm 84:5-7
59   Ezra 7:11-28
60   Matthew 28: 16-19; Mark 16:15-18

first task that Ezra had been commissioned to do, we see in the passage how the second task was meticulously completed:

> *On the fourth day, in the house of our God, we weighed out the silver and gold and the sacred articles into the hands of Meremoth son of Uriah, the priest. Eleazar son of Phinehas was with him, and so were the Levites Jozabad son of Joshua and Noadiah son of Binnui. Everything was accounted for by number and weight, and the entire weight was recorded at that time.*

(Ezra 8:33-34; NIV)

It begs the question of how meticulous are we in fulfilling the commission that God has given us. More importantly is the question of what our motivation is for doing so. If love is not at the core of the way we live our lives, then whatever we are doing will be motivated by something else. This means that we will not truly reflect our status as the children of God,[61] and as such, will be unable to touch the lives of those around us in the desired way since we are not living our lives in the light of our commitment to follow Jesus. In other words, when love is at the core of our lives, we will be living in such a way that we will not only want to fulfil the commission that God has given us but will do so in whatever way God has equipped us.

Returning to the story, we are now told about the sacrifices that the returning exiles made to the Lord. Once they had done that, they delivered the king's orders to those in authority in the Trans Euphrates area thus commissioning them to provide whatever assistance Ezra might need to ask them for.[62]

---

61   1 John 4:7-5:5
62   Ezra 8:35-36

The story now shifts away from the temple, as can be seen in the following verse:

After these things had been done, the leaders came to me and said, "The people of Israel, including the priests and the Levites, have not kept themselves from the neighbouring people with their detestable practices, like those of the Canaanites, Hittites, Perizzites, Jebusites, Ammonites, Moabites, Egyptians and Amorites.

(Ezra 9:1; NIV)

If you are not yet familiar with the Bible, you may struggle to understand not only what this is talking about but also the seriousness of what is being said. The detestable practices being spoken of here would have included idolatry, human sacrifices, and sexual immorality of a kind that probably would not be considered acceptable by most people living in today's world. Although the issue being spoken of was quite specific, as we will see in a moment, the basic point being made here is that God had given the people of Israel a clear framework concerning how He expected them to live, and they had not been doing it.

Even though we are not expected as Christians to follow a set of laws like the Old Covenant, we have been given a set of principles for our lives[63] and a guide to enable us to know how to apply them.[64] Ultimately, we are called to live a life fully reflecting what has been referred to as the royal law of love.[65]

Since it is what we have been commanded to do, obedience to it involves deciding to love in the way that has been asked of us. This kind of love is sacrificial and is not something we can

---

63   2 Timothy 3:16-17
64   John 16:13
65   Matthew 22:34-40

achieve in our strength. We need the help of the Holy Spirit. As we learn to partner with Him in our journey into God's heart for us, our whole way of living will change; love will be at the core of our lives,[66] and it will be visible in the way we live.

Returning to the story, we now read:

They have taken some of their daughters as wives for themselves and their sons and have mingled the holy race with the peoples around them. And the leaders and have led the way in this unfaithfulness.

(Ezra 9:2 NIV)

God had forbidden the people of Israel to intermarry with the peoples around them because He knew that if they did, they would no longer want to live the way in which He wanted them to.[67] However, they did not listen to Him, and this resulted in God lifting His hand of protection from them.

Although we have not been given such a rigid framework for our lives as the people of Israel were, we are still called to live differently from those who are not believers.[68] Our lives need to flow out of love; love for God, others, and ourselves.[69] This will be reflected in our values and lifestyle.[70] If we are doing so, this will be evident to those around us because we will look and 'smell' differently to those who do not know God the way we do.[71]

The fact that there were leaders leading the people astray should not surprise us because the same kind of thing has

---

66   1 John 4:8-21
67   Deuteronomy 7:1-6; Joshua 23:12-13
68   1 John 2:15-17
69   Matthew 22:34-40
70   1 John 3:16-20
71   2 Corinthians 2:14-16a

happened and is still happening in the life of the Church. Since we are all prone to doing things we should not be doing, we have no right to stand in judgement on leaders who have experienced some kind of moral failure.[72] In fact, our shared weakness and fallibility is one of the reasons we need to be praying for our leaders whose visibility sets them up for numerous spiritual attacks of various kinds.[73]

> *When I heard this, I tore my tunic and cloak and sat down appalled. Then everyone who trembled at the words of the God of Israel gathered round me because of this unfaithfulness of the exiles. And I sat there appalled until the evening sacrifice.*
>
> (Ezra 9:3-4; NIV)

Reading this part of the story reminded me of a situation that I was reluctantly brought into several years ago when I lived in London. It involved some rather poisonous gossip about a couple of people that I knew, and I was dragged into the situation when I became the recipient of what was being said. What I was told disgusted me and left me feeling sick at heart. I took what I had been told to my then pastor. Not only did the pastor in question speak to the people spreading the story, but he preached the most amazing message the following Sunday about gossiping the gospel rather than about each other.

---

72   John 8:1-11 note v7
73   1 Peter 5:8b

5

IDENTIFICATION AND CONFESSION

*Then, at the evening sacrifice, I rose from self-abasement,
with my tunic and cloak torn, and fell on my knees with my
hands spread out to the Lord my God and prayed: I am too
ashamed and disgraced to lift up my face to you, because our
sins are higher than our heads and our guilt has been reached
to the heavens*
(Ezra 9:5-6; NIV)

The first thing Ezra did after he had absorbed what he had been told was to pray. This begs the question of whether our first response would be to pray or rush into what we thought was the right strategy for dealing with the problem if we found ourselves in a similar situation? Someone mature in their faith will take the situation to God and ask Him to give them the wisdom to know what their part is in dealing with whatever the issue is. Such a person will then wait on God until they have received His answer to their prayer before they act. Having said this, I am conscious that hearing the voice of God is not something that necessarily comes easily to us; it is a journey. As such, we can sometimes end up getting things wrong, but we should not beat ourselves up about it because we know that – *in all things God works together for the good of those who love him* (Romans 8:28).

Ezra begins the prayer we are now going to discuss in detail by identifying himself with his people in their sin. This raises the question of how conscious we are of the consequences of our actions and whether we identify ourselves in the way that Ezra did with our community.

We now read that:

> *From the days of our ancestors until now, our guilt is great. Because of our sins, we and our kings and our priests have been subjected to the sword and captivity, to pillage and humiliation at the hand of foreign kings, as it is today.*

(Ezra 9:7; NIV)

Having identified himself with his people in their sin, Ezra now goes on to acknowledge to God the consequences of their disobedience. Being able to recognise the consequences of our actions and the willingness to take responsibility for them is a sign of maturity both as a person and as a believer. However, an even greater sign is the ability to recognise and do that in terms of our community. Being able to do this and pray in the way Ezra did, is an indication of our willingness to lay down our lives according to Jesus' expectation.[74]

---

74   Matthew 16:24-25, Philippians 2:1-11 note particularly v4

It is perhaps worth noting at this point that the more conscious we are of our sin, the more we will recognise our need of God, and the more we see that, the more we will want to crucify our flesh.[75] Paradoxically, the more we crucify our flesh, the more freedom we will have, and therefore, the more we will experience the abundant life that Jesus promised us.[76]

In this part of the prayer, we get another glimpse of how Ezra sees God:

But now, for a brief moment, the Lord our God has been gracious in leaving us a remnant and giving us a firm place in his sanctuary, and so God gives light to our eyes and a little relief in our bondage.

(Ezra 9:8; NIV)

Our picture of God is crucial because how we see Him will affect our ability to believe that He can answer our prayers. The 'bigger' our view of God, the greater will be our capacity to believe His ability to do the impossible in our lives and the lives of those around us.[77] The best way of increasing our understanding of the character and nature of God is through reading the Bible. This is because the history contained within it speaks about the way God dealt with people in the past, and it reveals what He is like.

Ezra continues by saying that:

Though we are slaves, our God has not forsaken us in the sight of the kings of Persia; he has granted us to make new life to rebuild

---

75   Luke 14:24-27
76   John 10:10
77   Matthew 19:25-26; Luke 1:37

the house of our God and repair its ruins and has given us a wall
of protection in Judah and Jerusalem.

(Ezra 9:9; NIV)

This part of the prayer shows us that even though the people
of Israel had been unfaithful to God, He had not completely
abandoned them. More than that, we glimpse not only His grace,
but also His goodness and mercy, and His willingness to give
them another chance. Whilst the prayer speaks of a literal wall
of protection; it is worth noting that God also provides those
who are in right relationship with Him the spiritual equivalent
as can be seen in Job 1:10 and 3:23.[78]

Ezra then goes on to make a more specific confession than
the one he made earlier:

But now our God, what can we say after this? For we have forsaken
the commands you gave through your servants the prophets when
you said:' The land you are entering to possess is a land polluted
by the corruption of its peoples. By their detestable practices they
have filled it with iniquity from one end to the other.'

(Ezra 9:10-11; NIV)

This clear admission from Ezra regarding the nature of the
sin of his people will undoubtedly resonate in most, if not all,
of our hearts in one way or another. There is much going on
around us that goes against the way in which God has called us
all to live in His Word, even sadly within His family, the Church.

Moreover, reading this part of the prayer has probably raised
all sorts of questions in our hearts regarding the reason or

---

78   See also Psalm 5:11

reasons God has allowed what is happening across the world at this moment in time. I think there are different reasons for different nations and communities. Not only that, I believe we need to see it as a wake-up call for the Church! I also know you may not see things quite the same way as I do. However, we can probably all agree that whatever we think the reason or reasons are, we need to be talking to God about our lives. We need to ask Him to speak to us not only as individuals but also in a corporate way about the situation we are currently facing.

Ezra continues with God's perspective on intermarriage with the people living around them:

> '..Therefore do not give your daughters in marriage to their sons or take their daughters for your sons. Do not seek a treaty of friendship with them at any time, that you may be strong and eat the good things of the land and leave it to your everlasting inheritance.'
>
> (Ezra 9:12; NIV)

Whilst the people of Judah were forbidden to intermarry with the peoples that lived around them, we are not explicitly forbidden to marry those who are not believers although it seems be implied in 2 Corinthians 6:14-15. Whilst there are undoubtedly marriages taking place within the Body of Christ that are not pleasing to God for other reasons discussing it in any detail would be outside the scope of this book. However, some comments will be made on this subject in the next chapter. It is crucial for us to understand what God's heart for marriage is, and the Bible has a lot to teach us about this.[79]

Although the passage being discussed speaks about marriage,

---

79   Ephesians 5:22-33

there is an underlying principle that applies to us as Christians just as much as it did to the people of Israel. The key to understanding what is being spoken of here can be found in 1 John 2:15-17 (NIV), which says:

Do not love the world or anything in the world. If anyone loves the world the love of the Father is not in him. For everything in the world – the cravings of sinful man, the lust of his eyes, and the boasting of what he has and does comes not from the Father but from the world. The world and its desires pass away but the man who does the will of God lives for ever.

Basically, what this passage is speaking of is the need for us as believers to live differently from the people in our community who do not yet know the Lord. In other words, to live in such a way that our lives reflect not only the principles of the Kingdom taught by Jesus but also those throughout the Bible. Doing so means that our values, attitudes, and behaviour will set us apart from those around us who do not yet know God in the way that we do. That, in turn, will open us up to questions and those who find our answers attractive will be drawn to God and therefore to us.[80]

In the next part of Ezra's prayer, we see once again the link between sin and its consequences:

What has happened to us is a result of our evil deeds and our great guilt, and yet, our God, you have punished us less than our sins deserved and given us a remnant like this. Shall we then break your commands again and intermarry with the peoples who commit

---

80   2 Corinthians 2:14-16a

such detestable practices? Would you not be angry enough with us to destroy us, leaving us no remnant or survivor?

(Ezra 9:13-14; NIV*)*

This acknowledgement of the consequences of sin made by Ezra should speak to us all on some level since no human that is living, or that has lived, have been or are sinless, apart from Jesus of course! We all know to our cost, the kind of price we will pay if we do something that is not right or if someone sins against us.

The questions Ezra poses are the kind of questions that probably most, if not all of us, have struggled with after we have blown it in some way. We have undoubtedly too all suffered with the guilt or pain that sin causes. Thankfully, God is more than willing not just to forgive us but also to heal our wounds—even if they have been self-inflicted.[81]

I struggled for years over the failures in one or two areas of my life. It was not until I realised that I needed to forgive myself for the things I had got wrong that I finally got free of it. I now generally work through any areas where I may need to forgive myself when I recognise that I have blown it so I rarely struggle for long with feelings of guilt now.

Up to this point, Ezra's prayer has been an almost pure confession, but he now goes from that into a brief moment of worship before passing comment on what he sees as being the position of the people of Judah in God's eyes as he draws it to a close:

Lord, the God of Israel, you are righteous! We are left this day as a

---

81   (Isaiah 53:3-6; Jeremiah 30:17)

remnant. Here we are before you in our guilt, though because of it not one of us can stand in your presence.

(Ezra 9:15; NIV)

Acknowledging the goodness of God is a vital part of the devotional life of any believer, not only in Ezra's time but also in ours. It is the foundational part of a life of faith and forms the bedrock for the worship of our God.

6

BUILDING GODLY RELATIONSHIPS

While Ezra was praying and confessing, weeping and throw-
ing himself down before the house of God, a large crowd of
Israelites – men, women and children – gathered round him.
They too wept bitterly. Then Shekaniah son of Jehiel ..., said to
Ezra, "We have been unfaithful to our God by marrying foreign
women from the peoples around us. But in spite of this, there is
still hope for us..."
(Ezra 10:1-2; NIV)

Praying in a public place is something rarely seen today, but this is not the only time in the Bible, we see it being done (although it seem that Jesus advocated that we should not do so[82]). It looks as if Ezra's motive in doing so was so that others would hear his prayer and it would speak to them. Assuming that is the case, we can see from this verse

---

Matthew 6:5-6

that it had a major impact on those listening. So much so that it evoked an acknowledgement from all those who gathered around Ezra of their unfaithfulness to God and by implication, to the covenant He had made with them.

We too are in a covenant relationship with God. However, even though the covenant the people of Israel had with God involved obedience to the numerous laws, ours is all about living according to Kingdom principles and love. The similarities do not stop there either since we too can be unfaithful to God by not loving in the way that He has called us to.[83] This, of course, has wider implications than our marriages as it is not just our spouses we are called to love.

Let us now look at the outworking of the corporate confession mentioned previously:

"Now let us make a covenant before God to send away all these women and their children, in accordance with the counsel of my Lord and those who fear the commands of our God. Let it be done according to the Law. Rise up, this matter is in your hands. We will support you so take courage and do it."

(Ezra 10:3-4; NIV)

What we have just read reveals that the people who made the confession were not merely agreeing with Ezra's prayer, but their hearts had been changed, and as a result, they wanted to put things right with God. If repentance is genuine, it will always result in a change of heart and mind, which result in taking whatever action is necessary in the light of the change of direction being made. The response of the people affirms

---

83   1 John 4:7-21; 3:16-20

genuine repentance since they were eager to put things right and wanted things to be done according to the Law.

It is worth noting at this point that marriage is also a covenant between the couple and God. However, if the couple were not supposed to be married in the first place, as was the case in this situation, that automatically nullifies the covenant they are trying to make. This is because God will not honour a covenant that is made in His name which is not based on the pattern He has ordained.[84]

The situation we are taking about illustrates how our decisions can affect the lives of others; it shows us how one sin leads to another, and the impact our actions can have on others. The men of Israel did not just sin against God; they also sinned against the women and their children.

The men who made the public confession not only wanted to put things right but were also prepared to support Ezra in the action needed for them to be able to do so. This again shows the fullness of their repentance:[85]

...Ezra rose up and put the leading priests and Levites and all Israel under oath to what had been suggested. And they took the oath. Then Ezra withdrew from before the house of God and went to the room of Jehonan son of Eliashib. While he was there, he ate no food and drank no water, because he continued to mourn over the sin of the exiles. (Ezra 10:5-6; NIV)

Whilst we occasionally use oaths today, they are not something we are as familiar with as would have been the case for the

---

84   Genesis 2:24; Ephesians 5:22-32; Hebrews 13:4
85   See Acts 19:11-20 for a New Testament story about repentance of this kind.

people of Judah. Consequently, it seems probable that their approach to this oath was probably far more meaningful and heartfelt than the oaths of today.

What is particularly interesting is how Ezra continued to grieve for the sin of his people even after the oath was taken. There could be all sorts of reasons for this. For example:

Ezra might have experienced something of God's grief over the sin of the men and the consequences of their actions on others.

His grief could have been about the consequences of the breaking up of the families created by the relationships in question upon the women and children.

It is also perhaps worth saying here that the grieving process in a person's life can be complicated by other factors in their personal history. If, for example, someone has recently lost a loved one, it could take them a long time to recover from the death of such an individual with whom they had enjoyed a close relationship.

Continuing with the story, we are now told that:

> *A proclamation was then issued throughout Judah and Jerusalem for all the exiles to assemble in Jerusalem. Anyone who failed to appear within three days would forfeit all his property, in accordance with the decision of the officials and elders, and would himself be expelled from the assembly of the exiles.*

> (Ezra 10:7-8; NIV)

This proclamation may seem to us to be something of an overreaction to the situation under discussion, but it shows the seriousness of those involved to deal with it. It begs the question of how seriously we see sin, not only in our own lives but also in the lives of those around us. The more we hate sin, the less we will tolerate it in our lives and the less we will believe that some sins are more acceptable than others.

The process of putting things right for the people of Israel was undoubtedly not only painful but also complicated for all those involved. Moreover, sorting things out took time as is evident in this story:

> *Within the three days, all the men of Judah and Benjamin had gathered in Jerusalem. And on the twentieth day of the ninth month, all the people were sitting before the House of God, greatly distressed by the occasion and by the rain.*
>
> (Ezra 10:9; NIV)

The same will be true of other serious situations, including the one that we are currently experiencing, even if there are no issues of sin involved. When the lockdown finishes, there will be a lot to be resolved, not just on a personal level, but also within the life of our church communities. Some issues will be relatively easy to resolve, others will not be so simple, and we need to be prepared for that. The key to dealing with the issues that we face is honesty and as we will see this is the approach Ezra takes:

> *When Ezra the priest stood up and said to them, "You have been unfaithful; you have married foreign women, adding to Israel's guilt. Now honour the Lord, the God of your ancestors, and do his will. Separate yourselves from the peoples around you and from your foreign wives."* (Ezra 10:8-9)

Being confronted with the truth of their situation would not have been easy for the men of Israel to deal with, but as we will now see they responded positively:

The whole assembly responded with a loud voice: "You are right! We must do as you say. But there are many people here so we cannot stand outside. Besides this matter cannot be taken care of in a day or two, because we have sinned greatly in this thing..."

(Ezra 10:12-13; NIV)

The truth about ourselves, other people, or situations that we find ourselves in can be hard to swallow. The pandemic and all that has, or is happening because of it, will inevitably throw up issues for all of us that will be difficult to face. Some of the issues will be obvious or straightforward; others will be far more complicated, but the key to all of them will lie in our relationship with God.

The willingness of the men of Israel to put things right and their recognition of the need to do things properly was greater than perhaps might have been expected. Although there was some opposition to what was happening, it was minimal as seen in this verse:

"...Let our officials act for the whole assembly. Then let everyone in our towns who has married a foreign woman come at a set time, until the fierce anger of our God is turned away from us." Only Jonathon son of Asahel and Jahzeiah son of Tikvah, supported by Meshullam and Shabbethai the Levite opposed this.

(Ezra 10:14-15; NIV)

The process suggested by these men was taken on board by the people, and over the next couple of months, the agreed separations took place.[86] For us, the process of returning to whatever normal is going to look like will undoubtedly take much longer than that, as there will certainly be more issues to be resolved. However, there is the likelihood that the key area of our lives we will all struggle with will be our relationships. The key to dealing with whatever issues we have to face will be prayer, but the starting point for working them through is that every individual we have problems with is someone that God loves, even if they do not yet know Him, just as He does us.

One of the things that has not yet been spoken about much is that what is happening is traumatic for us all; some, of course, greater than others. This is going to impact all our relationships in some way, and therefore, needs to be taken into consideration when we are working through whatever issues we will have to deal with.

---

86   Ezra 10:16-44

7

GRIEF AND INTERCESSION

In the month of Kislev in the twentieth year, whilst I was in
the citadel of Susa, Hanani, one of my brothers, came from
Judah with some other men, and I questioned them about the
Jewish remnant that had survived the exile, and also about
Jerusalem. They said to me, "Those who survived the exile
and are back in the province are in great trouble and disgrace.
The walls of Jerusalem are burnt down, and its gates have
been burned by fire."
(Nehemiah 1:1-3; NIV)

We have now reached the part of the story that involves Nehemiah, and the first thing we learn about him is that he is in exile. We are also told about a report he was given about his homeland. In fact, most of this chapter will be spent in looking at Nehemiah's response to it, but reading it has probably raised the question for all as to how we have responded to the regular news we are being given about the pandemic. We will look at this shortly, but before we do let us look what Nehemiah's immediate response was:

When I heard these things, I sat down and wept. For some days I mourned and fasted and prayed before the God of heaven.

(Nehemiah 1:4; NIV)

Nehemiah's immediate response to the news that he was given was one of grief, but it did not stop there. He went on to fast and pray into the situation that had been described to him over what seems to have been about four months.[87] This raises a variety of thoughts about our situation. Have we worked through our initial response to what is happening with God? If we have not done so yet, fear, panic, or grief may fill our hearts and lives making us feel completely helpless and powerless.[88] If we have, are we doing what Nehemiah did?

Our response to what is happening will be influenced by all sorts of factors from our history to our medical situation. If we are finding it difficult to respond positively to what is happening, it is nothing to beat ourselves up about. It may mean that what we need to be seeking God about is healing for ourselves, rather than praying into the ongoing situation. It is worth noting that Nehemiah starts his prayer with worship and that in doing so he gives us a model for ours:

Then I said:"Lord the God of heaven, the great and awesome God, who keeps his covenant of love with those who love him and keep

---

87   Nehemiah 2:1
88   These verses may be helpful to you if you are struggling with such feelings: 2 Timothy 1:7; Psalm 112:1-9 note v6-8

his commandments, let your ear be attentive and your eyes open to
hear the prayer your servant is praying before you day and night
for your servants, the people of Israel..."

(Nehemiah 1:5-6A; NIV)

From what is said, we get a glimpse of his heart as well as a thumbnail sketch of how he sees God. As stated earlier, if our understanding of the character and nature of God is 'too small', it will limit our faith and therefore rob us of the ability to believe God for the impossible in our lives, or other people.[89] Moreover, whilst reading the Word is an essential part of increasing our faith, it can also be beneficial to read stories of what God has done in other people's lives.

Another thing about Nehemiah's prayer worth commenting on is the way he mentions that he is praying day and night for his people. This speaks not only of the strength of his identification with his people but also the level of his faith in God. The parable of the persistent widow, given in Luke 18:1-8, speaks of the power of persistent prayer. Not only that, it also links it with faith. It may be helpful to remind ourselves, and others, of what has been called the P-U-S-H principle—pray until something happens, if we are looking to God for some kind of breakthrough for ourselves or others.

I prayed for the salvation of Bob, my daughter's father, for about a year before he was saved and yet God has responded in one way or another to some of my other prayers far more quickly than that. However, persistence in prayer when God has already said no to our request will not bring about what we desire as I have discovered over the years!

---

89   Luke 1:37; Matthew 19:25-26

Nehemiah now echoes Ezra's prayer of confession:

"I confess the sins that we Israelites, including myself and my father's family, have committed against you. We have acted very wickedly towards you. We have not obeyed the commands decrees and laws that you gave your servant Moses..."

(Nehemiah 1:6B-7; NIV)

If you are not already doing so, perhaps you should be praying in a similar sort of way for your nation?[90] Both identificational repentance and intercession can be extremely powerful as evident in the transformational videos produced by Sentinel Media.

From next part of the prayer, we can see that like Ezra, Nehemiah reminded God about His covenant promises to Israel:

"...Remember the instructions that you gave your servant Moses, saying, if you are unfaithful, I will scatter you among the nations, but if you return to me and obey my commands, then even if your exiled people are at the furthest horizon, I will gather them from there and bring them to the place that I have chosen as a dwelling for my name."

(Nehemiah 1:8-9; NIV)

Whilst Ezra spoke about the issue of intermarriage, Nehemiah takes a different approach; his emphasis was on God bringing back His people after their disobedience to Him had caused them to be scattered. This, of course, raises the question as to

---

90   2 Chronicles 7:14

whether disobedience to God is the reason that we too have been scattered in the way we have. Some Christians obviously believe that to be the case, while others see things differently. However, at the end of the day, we all need to work out our own salvation.[91]

Nehemiah continues by reminding God of how He brought His people out of Egypt and made them His own:

They are your servants and your people, whom you redeemed and saved by your mighty hand. Lord, let your ear be attentive to the prayer of this your servant and to the prayer of your servants who delight in revering your name. Give your servant success today.

(Nehemiah 1:10-11; NIV)

Sometimes, it is good to remind God of what He has done for us and to thank Him not only for that but also what He is doing and will do in our times with Him. Doing so will undoubtedly lead us into worship, thus opening us up to hearing His voice.

Nehemiah ends his prayer by asking God for success for something he was going to do that day, thus indicating that this prayer was probably the one he prayed at the end of the fasting and prayer spoken of earlier.

Perhaps here we need to define what the Bible calls success because it is not defined by position, power or even wealth— such things are the world's definition, not God's. To see what God calls success, let us look at the people who are defined as being the heroes of the faith in Hebrews 11:1-34. We have all heard of people like Abraham and Isaac, but there are also numerous others in the list whose names are less well known;

---

91   (Philippians 2:12-13)

for example, Barak[92] and Jephthah.[93] The criteria for success in God's eyes can thus be defined as obedience and faith, rather than material success.

Let us now look at the situation that Nehemiah prayed into:

In the month of Nisan in the twentieth year of King Artaxerxes, when wine was brought for him, I took the wine and gave it to the king. I had not been sad in his presence before, so the king asked me, "Why does your face look so sad when you are not ill? This can be nothing but sadness of heart.

(Nehemiah 2:1-2A; NIV)

Here,[94] we learnt that Nehemiah was the cup-bearer for the king, and we see him functioning in that role. His position would not only have meant that he served the king with wine but also that he tasted it prior to doing so to protect his monarch from being poisoned!

Regarding this day, it seems probable that Nehemiah intentionally allowed the grief and distress he was feeling regarding the situation of his people to show:

I was very much afraid, but I said to the king, "May the king live for ever! Why should my face not look sad when the city where my ancestors are buried lies in ruins, and its gates have been destroyed by fire?"

(Nehemiah 2:3; NIV)

This is because he needed the king to open the door for him to speak about it as it would have broken court protocol for

---

92   Judges 4:4-22
93   Judges 10:6-12:7
94   Nehemiah 1:2b

him to say anything without having been invited to. Breaking through our fear of something can look like an impossible task, but in this verse, we are given the primary key to achieve this. Nehemiah had put his trust in God and was then able to speak freely to the king about the situation that was troubling him. The response he got was an extremely favourable one. The king, in fact, even asked him what he wanted.[95] The verse that follows describes his response:

> *Then I prayed to the God of heaven, and I answered the king, "If it pleases the king and if your servant has found favour in his sight, let him send me to the city in Judah where my ancestors are buried so that I can rebuild it."*
>
> (Nehemiah 2:4B; NIV)

Here, there is another indication of Nehemiah's trust in God and how that enabled him to do what he believed God wanted him to do. The way in which Nehemiah framed his request shows his deference towards the king. It also makes plain his status as a servant.

King Artaxerxes once again responded favourably and asked him how long the work would take and when he will return. Nehemiah sets a time which interestingly is not specified:[96]

> *I also said to him, "If it pleases the king, may I have letters to the governors of the Trans-Euphrates, so they will provide me safe conduct until I arrive in Judah? Also, may I have a letter to Asaph, keeper of the royal park, so he will give me timber to make beams,*

---

95   Nehemiah 2:4a
96   Nehemiah 2:6

for the gates of the citadel and for the city wall and for the residence I will occupy?

(Nehemiah 2:7-8A; NIV)

These verses show us that Nehemiah had worked out in advance what was needed for him to be able to do the work God had laid on his heart. For the situation we are in, such forward planning is not, and will not be possible because there are all too many unknown factors involved. This is why it is so vital for us to seek God for His wisdom and strategy for what we are and will be facing.

We are told that King Artaxerxes agreed to these requests, something Nehemiah interprets as being God's favour on him. Shortly after, the beginnings of the opposition he will later face awoken,[97] something we will speak of later in the book.

---

97   Nehemiah 2:8b-10

8

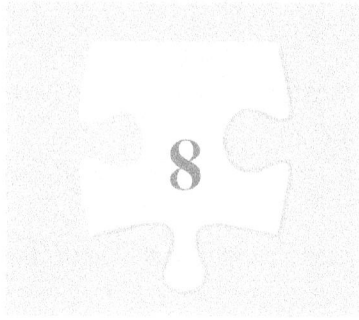

ASSESSING THE DAMAGE

I went to Jerusalem, and after staying there three days I set out during the night with a few others. I had not told anyone what my God had put in my heart to do for Jerusalem. ...By night I went out through the Valley Gate towards the Jackal Well and the Dung Gate, examining the walls of Jerusalem, which had been broken down and its gates, which had been destroyed by fire.

(Nehemiah 2:11-12A;13; NIV)

Three days after he got to Jerusalem, Nehemiah went out during the night to assess the level of damage that had been done to the walls of the city when it had been sacked years before. It is unlikely that anyone is going to come out of the current situation without having had their lives damaged in some way. Still, it is also probable that not all the damage done will show immediately. This means that while making an assessment will enable us to start praying into and planning for our future, those plans will need to be flexible to allow for the unknown factors.

When he went to make that assessment, Nehemiah did not make his intentions known to many people,[98] although he did take a couple with him. This shows great wisdom and gives us two fundamental principles we can apply to our own lives. The first is not to be too open about our plans for the future; the second is not to keep things entirely to ourselves as we do need people to talk to who can encourage or support us in different ways.[99]

A particularly good example of such support is the way Aaron and Hur held up Moses' hands when the Israelites were in the middle of a battle. This gives us such a powerful picture of what support looks like. Whenever Moses grew tired and was no longer able to hold up his hands, the other two men held them up for him, speaking of not only practical support, but also intercession.[100]

We may not have individuals that can provide the high level of support we may need when we are facing difficulties or in times of crisis. However, we may be able to get different aspects of it from different people or perhaps even organisations. Moreover, we as individuals may not be able to provide all the help those around us in such situations need, but we may be able to provide part of it. If people come to us for help, we need to be asking God for His guidance in our response to that person, rather than perhaps promising support and then not giving it or sending them away empty-handed.

Nehemiah's assessment of the situation seems to have been

---

98   Nehemiah 2:16
99   Proverbs 27:9
100   Exodus 17:8-15

very thorough which is again something we can all learn from:

Then I moved on towards the Fountain Gate and the King's Pool,
but there was not enough room for my mount to get through, so I
went up the valley by night, examining the wall. Finally, I turned
back and re-entered through the Valley Gate.

(Nehemiah 2:14-15; NIV)

The temptation to assess a situation or a person for that matter, by making assumptions based on what is immediately obvious, is strong. However, such a superficial approach could eventually cause us all sorts of problems as well as perhaps creating difficulties for other people. In this season, we have probably not reached the point of being able to assess the damage that has been done to our lives, although we may be aware of some of it. It would, therefore, be unwise to make concrete plans until we have a much clearer picture of the situation.

We should instead start praying into the areas of our lives that we are already aware have been damaged, asking God for healing or restoration as appropriate. We can also ask God for fresh hope, vision, wisdom, strategy, and direction for the season that is coming.

In this story, let us see what Nehemiah said to the Priests, nobles, officials, and all those who would be doing the work on the wall:

...I said to them, "You see the trouble that we are in; Jerusalem
lies in ruins, and its gates have been burned with fire. Come, let
us rebuild the wall of Jerusalem, and we will not be in disgrace. I
also told them about them about the gracious hand of my God on

me and what the king had said to me." They replied, "Let us start
rebuilding." So they began this good work.

(Nehemiah 2:17-18; NIV)

Nehemiah's approach to the people of the city enabled them to
see the situation as being one that affected them all and brought
them together as a group. Not only that, his approach united
them behind the vision to rebuild the walls, thus giving them
hope and vision, something that will be of vital importance in
not just rebuilding our lives but also our communities.

None of us are going to be able to rebuild our lives without
some input from other people, and rebuilding our communities
is going to require us to work together as one. For us to be able
to work effectively with others indicate that we will have to work
through any wrong heart attitudes, which might hinder us from
being able to do so with God. We may, for example, need to work
through our attitude to a particular thing or even a group of
people. Not only that, we may also need to work through our
history with specific individuals because forgiveness opens the
door for healing, something that we will all need on some level
as the work of rebuilding begins.

Soon enough, we now begin to see the rise of the opposition
that was mentioned in the Book towards the people of Judah:

...when Sanballat the Horonite, Tobiah the Ammonite official
and Geshem the Arab heard about it they mocked and ridiculed
us. "What is this you are doing?" They asked. "Are you rebelling
against the king?"

(Nehemiah 2:19; NIV)

Earlier on in the chapter, we were told that Sanballat, Tobiah, and Geshem did not want anyone *to promote the welfare of the Jewish people*[101] and now we see them opposing the rebuilding of the walls of Jerusalem. This begs the question of whether they were prejudiced because it certainly looks as if they were but since the bible does not tell us we cannot be certain.

Moreover, as it has been said before, whenever we press into God's purposes for our lives and start to move forward in them, we will most probably face an opposition of some kind. As we begin to break out of lockdown, there are bound to be voices of dissension and quite probably other forms of opposition too, because:

Your enemy the devil prowls around like a roaring lion looking for someone to devour. (1 Peter 5:8B; NIV)

Most of the time, the opposition that we face is relatively easy to deal with, but at times it can be far more complicated. Whatever the case, we need to seek God for the right strategy for the situation we are facing, because occasionally, the answer to whatever situation we are facing is simpler than we think it is. This is something that was demonstrated in quite a remarkable way in the story of the two Arameans given in 2 Kings 6:8-23. What is done in that story contrasts sharply the story of the fall of Jericho,[102] which speaks about a rather different kind of strategy. Some would call the strategy used at Jericho a form of warfare but would not necessarily consider what happened with the two Arameans as one. How we see such things all depends

---

101   Nehemiah 2:10
102   Joshua 6:1-25

on our perspective; we need to see things through God's eyes rather than ours.

Moving on now to the response Nehemiah gave to the men that were opposing the rebuilding of the walls:

I answered them by saying, "The God of heaven will give us success. We his servants will start rebuilding, but as for you, you have no share in Jerusalem or any claim or right to it."

(Nehemiah 2:20; NIV)

From this verse, the strength and depth of Nehemiah's faith in God are evident. Such strong faith indicates a person who has learnt what it means to depend on God and live their lives in the light of that. More than that, it is one of the signs of spiritual maturity because we do not begin our journey into God's heart for us with that level of faith.

The confidence Nehemiah had in God concerning what he was doing gave him the boldness to speak against those who were opposing him. The same will be true for us in our lives when we know that we are doing what God has called us to do. This is why it is so vital for us to develop our relationship with God. The process of rebuilding the walls of Jerusalem has so much to teach us, not just about the restoration of our lives and the rebuilding of our communities, but also about our relationship with God and the journey of faith.

The ten gates, in the next chapter, give us a picture of the progressive development of the life of a believer, and thus, have an application to Church as a whole. The gates can, therefore, be used as reminders for us of how we are to live as believers and as part of the family of God.

The walls, on the other hand, picture how we as believers are called to separate ourselves from 'the world,' to be in it yet not part of it. The following verses shed light on this matter and clearly show us what God expects of us:

> *Do not love the world or anything in the world. If anyone loves the world, love for the Father is not in them. For everything in the world - the lust of the flesh, the lust of the eyes and the pride of life come not from the Father but from the world. The world and its desires pass away, but whoever does the will of God lives forever.*
>
> (1 John 2:15-17; NIV)

In other words, we are called to live differently to those who do not yet know God the way we do. In practical terms, this means we do not necessarily share in the kind of lifestyle or values such people espouse, but instead, look at the principles of the Kingdom for guidance on the way God wants us to live.

It is perhaps worth noting here that only those who were able to prove their Jewish ancestry were, in fact, allowed to be involved in the rebuilding of the walls. For us, that is a picture of what it means to be in Christ[103] because only those who are true believers are part of the Church which is His body.[104] The gates are thus a picture of being in the world but not of it. Not only that, but some have also seen the gates as being a representation of the responsibility that we have towards God and others.

Some of you are probably asking at this point where that thought comes from, and the answer has to do with the significance of the number of gates in the wall. This is because the

---

103   Ephesians 1:4-14
104   1 Corinthians 12:12-27

number ten can be interpreted as being the number associated with personal responsibility. The basis for this has to do with the Ten Commandments, which were written on two stone tablets; the commandments represent the way God expects us to behave towards Himself and those around us.

9

KEYS TO REBUILDING AND RESTORING (PART 1)

Eliashib the High Priest and his fellow priests went to work and rebuilt the Sheep Gate. They dedicated it and set its doors in place, building as far as the Tower of the Hundred, which they dedicated, and as far as the Tower of Hananel. The men of Jericho built the adjoining section, and Zakur son of Imri built next to them.

(Nehemiah 3:1-2; NIV)

T he fact that Nehemiah starts his account of the rebuilding of the walls with the sheep gate was no accident as Jesus is our Passover lamb,[105] and it is through His sacrifice that we become part of God's family, the Church. Not just that, the name *Eliashib* means *God restores*, and the story of salvation is one of restoration. Seeking healing for ourselves and others

---

105   Exodus 12:1-23; John 1:29

should, therefore, be seen as an essential part of our journey into God's heart, not just individually, but also corporately.

We are not told whether it was Nehemiah who arranged and allocated the works to be done by individuals on the walls of the city, but it is certainly implied. If we want to be successful in Kingdom terms, there will inevitably be a process involved, and in these verses, we see a picture of that in the requirements for rebuilding the city's walls.

It is perhaps worth noting here that in John 10:1-18, Jesus speaks of being the gate for the sheep before speaking of Himself as the Good Shepherd.[106] The sheep gate was the gate through which animals were brought in from the countryside for sacrifice. Once in the city, there was only one other door through which the sheep were taken before being sacrificed. Knowing this increases our understanding of the following verses:

"I am the gate; whoever enters through me will be saved. They will come in and go out, and find pasture. The thief comes only to steal, kill and destroy: I have come that they may life, and have it to the full."

(John 10:9-10; NIV)

These verses referred to what was mentioned earlier in the book as being the rest of faith.[107] It is vital for us all to recognise that we will never be able to enter this rest until we stop trying to work everything out for ourselves because it is from there we will enter into the abundant life God desires to give us.[108]

For us to be able to enter our Promised Land, we need to

---

106   John 10:11
107   Hebrews 4:1-11
108   Jeremiah 29:11

progressively surrender our lives to God,[109] including whatever plans we are making for the future and allow Him to show us His. This is because what God has for us will be infinitely better than anything that we have planned for ourselves.[110]

The Fish Gate in the Book of Nehemiah speaks of Jesus and it is perhaps worth noting that the outline of His name in New Testament Greek forms the symbol of a fish:

The Fish Gate was rebuilt by the sons of Hassenaah. They laid the beams and put its doors and bolts and bars in place. Meremoth son of Uriah, the son of Hakkoz, repaired the next section. Next to him Meshullam, the son of Meshazzabel, made repairs, and next to him Zadok son of Baana also made repairs.

(Nehemiah 3:3-4; NIV)

Moreover, Jesus implies that He is a fisherman when He calls Simon and Andrew to be His disciples because He tells them that He is going to make them fishers of men.[111] This is something that all who claim to be His disciples are called to do,[112] although how we do so will depend on the abilities and gifts He has given us.

In the work that was done on the walls each person involved had a specific part to play, and the same will be true of us regarding the rebuilding of our communities. The Church is described as a body in 1 Corinthians 12:12-27, and in that, we see a wonderful picture of part of God's blueprint for church life. We need to recognise that we are all needed in different

---

109   Romans 12:1
110   Jeremiah 29:11
111   Mark 1:16-18
112   Matthew 28:16-20

ways for our communities to be able to function properly and thrive. In other words, each person in our community has an important part to play in its life so they are of inestimable value and worth. However, there are always going to be those who are not willing to play their part as exemplified in the next verse of the story:

The next section was repaired by the men of Tekoa, but their nobles would not put their shoulders to the work under supervision.

(Nehemiah 3:5; NIV)

The nobles mentioned here were unwilling to do what was being asked of them, but the vast majority did. We should all know that there are going to be people who are not team players and will refuse to play their part in rebuilding what is supposed to be their community. There are also going to be some who do not seem to know that God has called them for a purpose, and it involves using their gifts, etc., to do the work of the Kingdom. Not only that, there will those who have been badly traumatised by all that has happened to them during the pandemic and will need to be dealt with sensitively. We need to be careful therefore not to assume that people are being difficult when we recognise their lack of involvement and ensure that if we challenge them about their attitude we do so for the right reasons.[113]

The Jeshanah Gate was rebuilt by the Joida son of Paseah and Meshullam son of Bosodeiah. They laid its beams and put its doors and bolts and bars in place. Next to them repairs were made

---

113   Matthew 7:1-2

by men from Gibeon and Mizpah – Melatiah of Gibeon and Jadon of Meronoth – places under the authority of the governor of the Trans-Euphrates.

(Nehemiah 3:6-7; NIV)

The word *Jeshanah* means *old*, and it signifies the need to return to the old ways of doing things:[114] One of the hallmarks of revival, from a biblical perspective, involves the restoration of biblical truth in terms of moral and doctrinal practice.[115] Those working on the wall give us a picture of what this looks like in practice. This is because they came from all walks of life,[116] thus showing us that the maintaining of biblical standards is something all of us can, and should, be involved in. This, of course, is something that needs to flow out of our love for God and others,[117] rather than out of what is best described as being misguided religious zeal.[118]

Rebuilding our lives and communities so that they will thrive will require us to be certain that we are building them on a firm foundation and that means that we need to be certain that we are using the plumb line of truth properly to do so.[119]

The Valley Gate was repaired by Hanun and the residents of Zanoah. They rebuilt it and put its doors with their bolts and bars in place. They also repaired a thousand cubits of the wall as far as the Dung Gate.

(Nehemiah 3:13; NIV)

---

114   Jeremiah 6:16a
115   2 Kings 22:1-23:30
116   Nehemiah 3:8-12
117   1 John 5:1-5
118   Matthew 15:1-9
119   Matthew 7:24-27

If you went out of the city through the Valley Gate, it would take you to the Valley of Hinnom, which was a place that was used for pagan worship at some point in the history of Israel as given in the Bible. A valley is a low place, and some valleys are difficult places to gain access to. Hence, what is said by David in Psalm 23:4 which speaks of walking through *the valley of the shadow of death* is not an overstatement.

Since a shadow is a projection caused by the way light is reflecting things, someone or something on a surface of some kind, the Valley Gate can, therefore, be seen as representing the death of self that was spoken of as being essential for all those who want to follow Jesus.[120] This, of course, was not just something Jesus spoke but what He modelled for us throughout His life.[121] Humility was the hallmark of Jesus' earthly life and it should be ours too,[122] not just individually but corporately.

The church community we are part of can demonstrate humility in two ways:

- By how we serve each other so that those who visit us who do not yet have a relationship with God will see Him reflected in the way we care for one another,[123] and
- By how we serve the wider community in different ways.[124]

The Dung Gate was repaired by Malkijah son of Rekab, ruler of the district of Beth Hakkerem. He rebuilt it and put the doors with their bolts and bars in place. (Nehemiah 3:14; NIV)

---

120   Luke 9:23-25; 14:25-27
121   Mark 10:45
122   Philippians 2:5-11
123   1 John 3:16-18
124   Matthew 25:31-46

If you were looking for the City dump, you would need to go out through the Dung Gate to get to it. A city the size of Jerusalem needed to have a place outside of it for people to take their rubbish to keep it clean. The Dung Gate is a picture for us as individuals or groups to engage holiness, a subject that is not often spoken about today.

The problem is that too many people think of holiness as being about God wanting to stop us from enjoying ourselves, but that is not so. God hates it when we do something wrong, primarily because in doing such things, we damage ourselves and others. Think for a second of two people who get embroiled in an affair. If they are both married, and each has two children, that affair is going to affect, at least, six other people and probably more.

However, before we go any further, we need to remember that there are two different but inseparably connected aspects of holiness; the first is usually referred to as justification while the second is known as sanctification.

Justification speaks of our legal righteousness. In other words, the moment we become Christians, our sin is covered, and our eternal destiny is now secure. This means our sin is no longer a barrier stopping us from being promoted to heaven after our earthly life ends.

On the other hand, sanctification is the process by which we become experientially holy. Whenever we sin once we have confessed it[125] the Holy Spirit is then able to work repentance into our hearts, changing us from the inside out. Another aspect of the work of sanctification is what many refer to as being inner

---

125   1 John 1:5-10

healing,[126] and this again is something that we do in partnership with the Holy Spirit. His role in this area of our lives is that of inner transformation, progressively enabling us to become more like Jesus.[127] This work of transformation is what enables us to become effective witnesses[128] and point people to Jesus.

However, just as a lack of holiness can negatively impact our individual witness, so the same is true of our church communities. Would someone walking into the church at Corinth in Paul's time have seen anything to draw them into a relationship with God? While the answer is probably yes because salvation is a work of the Spirit, such an individual could nevertheless be negatively affected by some of the things Paul mentioned in his first letter to the church, which may make it more difficult for them to surrender their lives to God. If you are not familiar with this letter now might be a good time to read it.

Our church communities need to be places where people not only experience the love of God in how we care for each other, but also to see the difference our faith has made in the way we live our lives as a community. Outsiders will then see that the gospel is good news and want to become part of the family of God.

---

126   Isaiah 61:1-3
127   2 Corinthians 3:17-18; Galatians 5:22-24
128   Matthew 28:18-20; Acts 1:1-8 note v8

10

KEYS TO REBUILDING AND RESTORING (PART 2)

The Fountain Gate was repaired by Shallum son of Kol-Hozeh, ruler of the district of Mizpah. He rebuilt it, roofing it over and putting its doors and bolts and bars in place. He also repaired wall of the pool of Siloam, by the King's Garden, as far as the steps going down from the City of David.

(Nehemiah 3:15; NIV)

B efore we discuss the significance of the gate, we need to speak about the pool of Siloam, since the two are connected. During the period some describe as His earthly ministry, Jesus sent a blind man to the pool of Siloam to wash his eyes after He had put mud on them. He did so, and a miracle took place—he was able to see for the first time in his life.[129] It is noteworthy that the meaning of Siloam is *sent*, and the reason for that will become clear shortly.

---

129   John 9:1-7

The Fountain Gate is a picture of what some would call the overflow of the Spirit in our lives, more commonly referred to as the baptism in the Holy Spirit.[130] It is Jesus[131] who sends the Holy Spirit into our hearts and lives. His role is not only to take us through the salvation process but to empower us to be the witnesses we are called to be.[132] Through the baptism in the Spirit, we have access to the gifts[133] and offices[134] that are needed to equip us to fulfil the Great Commission[135] in whatever way we have been called to do so as individuals.[136]

I still remember how excited I was when I went to what was my first meeting as a Christian and saw some of the gifts of the Spirit being used. Having read the Book of Acts when I was at school, I immediately recognised what they were. In fact, I can remember saying to someone that what I was seeing was straight out of the Book of Acts!

We live in a time and day when spiritual gifts are not being recognised or encouraged in the way they once were even in Pentecostal circles. Yet these gifts are a vital part of the spiritual health of our church communities so there needs to be enough freedom in our meetings to enable people to operate in them. Moreover, we need to have workshops as we did years ago to teach and train people on how to use them well.

The gate described next is a picture of the Word of God:

---

130   Acts 19:1-7
131   Luke 3:16
132   Acts 1:4-8
133   1 Corinthians 12:4-8
134   Ephesians 4:11-13
135   Matthew 28:18-20
136   Ephesians 2:10

Next to him, Binnui son of Hadad repaired another section, from
Azariah's house to the angle and corner, and Palal son of Uzzai
worked opposite the angle projecting from the upper Palace near
the courtyard of the guard. Next to him, Pedaiah and the temple
servants living on the hill of Ophel made repairs up to a point
opposite the Water Gate towards the east and the projecting tower.

(Nehemiah 3:24-26; NIV)

This is because it is spoken of as being like water in a variety
of different ways in the Bible. However, before we look at a
couple of passages about that let us look at one key passage
that speaks about power of the Word itself:

As the rain and snow come down from heaven and do not return
to it without watering the earth and making it bud and flourish,
so that it yields seed for the sower and bread for the eater, so is
my word that goes out from my mouth: it will not return to me
empty but will accomplish what I desire and achieve the purpose
for which I sent it.

(Isaiah 55:10-11; NIV)

The quotation just given will enlarge and illuminate our understanding of the two examples of the Word being compared to
water that we are now going to discuss briefly. The first one can
be found in John 3:1-7[137] where Jesus is talking to Nicodemus
about the new birth. Jesus speaks of it as taking place not only
through water but also the Spirit. From this and the preceding
quotation, we can see that the Word and the breath, or Spirit
of God, cannot be completely separated. Both are needed for

---

137   See also I Peter 1:23

the releasing of the supernatural power of God into a life or situation, for it to be transformed.

This is evident too in our second example, which can be found in Ephesians 5:25-27 where it speaks of the cleansing of the Church with the water of the Word. The process involved is to prepare us for not just doing the work of the Kingdom but also to be part of what will be the greatest celebration of love that has ever happened.[138]

Understanding and appropriately applying the principles of the Kingdom given to us in the Word[139] will be vital as we pray for and work towards rebuilding our lives and church communities after the pandemic is over.

Above the Horse Gate, the priests made repairs, each in front of his own house.

(Nehemiah 3:28; NIV)

The Horse Gate was the one that was strategically placed near the stables and Palace. This meant that the king was able to mobilise the army and get them out of the city very quickly if necessary. For us, therefore, it reveals the war between the Kingdom of Light and the kingdom of darkness[140] that we as believers are caught up in. A good picture of what we are saying is given in Daniel 10:13, which shows us an answer to prayer being delayed for twenty-one days. There is another, and somewhat different example in Acts 16:22-26, involving a miraculous escape from prison; the fall of Jericho[141] is, of course, another.

---

138   Revelation 19:6-9
139   James 1:22-25
140   Ephesians 6:12
141   Joshua 6:1-25

Spiritual warfare takes many forms, but the key to the breakthrough that we are looking for ourselves or others lies in partnering with the Spirit and being guided by Him in our prayers. While more will be said in the next chapter on this subject, this is an area of teaching that has fallen out of favour in recent years, yet a good understanding of it is vital for our growth and well-being as a believer. Not only do we need it for our own protection, but it is essential for us in the rebuilding of our church communities.

Next to them, Zadok son of Immer made repairs opposite his house. Next to him, Shemaiah son of Shekaniah, the guard at the East Gate made repairs.

(Nehemiah 3:29; NIV)

According to Ezekiel 43:1-7 when Jesus returns to take His throne, He will enter Jerusalem through the East Gate, so this gate is both a picture and a reminder of the hope that that gives us. However, before we look at this any further, we need to speak briefly about what is referred to as the rapture of the Church.[142] This is because whilst some do not see that as being a separate event from the Second Coming there does not appear to be any way of reconciling the two events, but to go into this in any detail would be outside the scope of this book.

There are several key passages that describe the Second Coming in some detail but the one that describes the signs that will accompany it in the most detail is probably Matthew 24:1-51. The signs spoken of include things such as false Christs, wars, rumours of wars, earthquakes; all of which we have seen

---

142   1 Thessalonians 4:16-17

in plenty in recent years. This has meant over the years there have a lot of ideas put forward about this prophecy and others like it. The reality is that whilst there are aspects of end time prophecy that are easily understood there is a lot more that is not. However, since we are talking about essential truths that will give people hope that one day they will be with God, it is vital that there is a certain amount of discussion and teaching about them in our church communities.

Next to him, Malkijah, one of the goldsmiths, made repairs as the house of the temple servants and the merchants, opposite the Inspection Gate and as far as the room above the corner, and between the room above the corner and the Sheep Gate the gold-smiths and merchants made repairs.

(Nehemiah 3:31-32 NIV)

The Hebrew word that is translated here as Inspection is *miphkad*. In the NRSV the gate is referred to as being the Muster Gate which can be interpreted as meaning a place of review. Some think that it may have been the place where the religious leaders of the time, the Sanhedrin, tried cases. It seems that it was probably a place of judgement. This gate is therefore a picture for us of the final judgement.

Although no true believer will face what is referred to as being the Great White Throne,[143] because we have accepted the gift of salvation,[144] we will nevertheless face another form of judgement. We will not be judged on our sin but on how we lived for God. The purpose of this judgement is to reward us

---

143   Revelation 20:11-15
144   John 3:16-18

appropriately for the things we have done that are of spiritual consequence.[145] This is another area of teaching that has fallen out of favour for various reasons, and yet, it gives the believer the hope of receiving an eternal reward for all they have done for the Kingdom. We must recognise its importance and ensure it is taught in our church communities.

It is perhaps worth noting that all the gates were connected by the wall, which is a picture representing for us the kind of the protection that will be produced by a healthy church community for its members. To put it another way, our church communities should be places of security and safety for all those who are part of them. This will flow not only out of our love for God but also for one another.[146] Our relationships are, therefore, a vital part of rebuilding not only our lives but also our church communities. If we have issues with other believers, we need to work them through with God,[147] and if possible, with them.[148]

---

145   1 Corinthians 3:12-15; 2 Corinthians 5:10b
146   1 Corinthians 12:12-26 note particularly v24b-26
147   Ephesians 4:2-3
148   Matthew 18:15-17

11

THE BATTLE BEGINS

*When Sanballat heard that we were rebuilding the wall, he
became very angry and was greatly incensed. He ridiculed the
Jews, and in the presence of his associates and the army of
Samaria, he said, "What are those feeble Jews doing? Will they
restore their wall? Will they finish in a day? Can they bring the
stones back to life from those heaps of rubble?"*

(Nehemiah 4:1-2; NIV)

Insecure people tend to see other people's potential success
as a threat to them, and that is what Sanballat's attitude
here suggests. Such an attitude creates jealousy and spite
which can be incredibly destructive if allowed free reign. The
kind of remarks made by Sanballat and Tobiah[149] also indicate
not only prejudice but extreme animosity, especially when
viewed in the light of earlier comments made about him.[150]

---

149   Nehemiah 4:3
150   Nehemiah 2;10;19

People with such an attitude can be rather difficult to deal with. While we should always seek reconciliation with people if possible, we need to recognise that there are some situations where it may not happen.

The prayer that follows shows us how the people felt about what was happening:

Hear, O our God, for we are despised. Turn their insults back on their own heads. Give them over as plunder in a land of captivity. Do not cover up their guilt or blot out their sins from your sight, for they have thrown insults in the face of the builders.

(Nehemiah 4:4-5; NIV)

However, this is not the way in which we should be praying in the light of the teaching that Jesus gave us about loving even our enemies.[151] Having said that, when we pray we need to be honest about how we feel, including things and the situations we find ourselves in. This is because we are called to walk in the light,[152] and it is only when we do so that we can be set free because truth is the vehicle of our freedom. Moreover, God knows us intimately and is fully aware of our situation, so it is pointless putting any sort of a spin on things!

Returning to the story we see what happened did not stop the work[153] and that:

...when Sanballat, Tobiah, the Ammonites and the people of Ashdod heard that the repairs to the walls of Jerusalem had gone ahead and that the gaps were being closed they were very angry.

---

151   Luke 6:27-36; James 2:12
152   1 John 1:5-7
153   Nehemiah 4:6

They all plotted together to come and fight against Jerusalem and stir up trouble against it.

(Nehemiah 4:7-9; NIV)

This kind of reaction is often associated with the sort of situation we are talking about. It does not make it right for us to behave in the way that is described. While it is not wrong for us to be angry, we need to learn how to channel it appropriately.[154] The response of the group building the wall is one that we can learn a lot from in dealing with whatever life throws at us:

...we prayed to our God and posted a guard day and night to meet this threat.

(Nehemiah 4:10; NIV)

Before taking any action ourselves when things go wrong, the best thing we can do is to pray. In doing so, we are inviting God into the situation, which will change the way we deal with it as well as allowing Him to speak into whatever is going on. Again, it enables us to grow in our ability to trust in terms of our relationship with God, as we are then entrusting our lives to Him on a deeper level.

While the action taken by these men was obvious, that will not always be the case for us regarding our lives or the situations we are involved in. If we partner with the Holy Spirit in seeking God's heart for us, then He can give us the needed wisdom and strategies for the different things we might face.[155]

Now, we are told that the opposition took its toll on those

---

154   Ephesians 4:26-27
155   Romans 12:2-3

working on the wall and further threats were made.[156] Nehemiah then describes his response to all of this:

> *...I stationed some of the people behind the lowest points of the wall at the exposed places, posting them by families, with their swords, spears, and bows.*
>
> (Nehemiah 4:13; NIV)

Nehemiah takes what was probably the best action given the circumstances he was facing. However, in Nehemiah's day, they would not have had access to the whole Bible as most of it was not yet written. This means that the response we see in these two verses we are looking at would have come entirely out of his understanding of the situation. We have access not just to the complete Bible, but also to God Himself in a way that Nehemiah did not. Consequently, we know for example that our fight is not against the people involved; our arena of battle is in the spiritual realm,[157] and we need to partner with the Holy Spirit to the maximum in order to win the battle. Once we have done that, every victory we win will then be manifested here on earth. This, by the way, does not sadly mean we will win every battle because all sorts of variables come into play, including God's purpose and will for our lives. In such situations, we need to thank God that He is working things out for our good, according to Romans 8:28-29, and keep on looking to Him for the future.

We also need to recognise that:

---

156   Nehemiah 4:10-11
157   Ephesians 6:12

...though we live in the world we do not wage war as the world does. The weapons that we fight with are not the weapons of the world. For though we live in the world we do not wage war as the world does. On the contrary they have divine power to demolish strongholds.

(2 Corinthians 10:3-4; NIV)

Of course, this changes how we deal with difficult situations, because it means that we do not go into interpersonal conflicts all guns blazing. Instead, we use our God-given authority and pray into the situation in whatever way we feel led, using the weapons He has given us. For those of you who are new to the faith or uncertain as to what those are, the main ones are listed below:

- Praying whatever scriptures God [158] gives us as we seek His guidance regarding how to pray for a particular situation can be life-changing for the people we are praying for and for us.

- Using the name of Jesus in our prayers can also bring about a breakthrough in our lives or of those around us.[159]

- Praise can be incredibly powerful, resulting in miracles happening not only in our lives but also in the lives of others.[160]

- Praying in agreement with other believers can also bring about an intervention by God in a situation that seems

---

158   Ephesians 6:17-18
159   Acts 3:1-10
160   Acts 12:1-12

intractable,[161] particularly when the prayers line up with known Kingdom principles.

- Using what is often referred to as the principle of binding and loosing can be used to bring about God's purposes in a situation too.[162]

Now let us look at how Nehemiah responded to the opposition that was troubling those building the wall so much:

After I looked things over, I stood up and said to the nobles, the officials and the rest of the people, "Don't be afraid of them. Remember the Lord, who is great and awesome, and fight for your families, your sons and your daughters, your wives and your homes."

(Nehemiah 4:14; NIV)

We all need encouragement, particularly during difficult seasons in our lives. Nehemiah recognised that those working on the wall were feeling discouraged, and he spent time giving them some encouragement. Good leaders will always recognise the needs of those whom God has given them responsibility for. More importantly, they will do what they feel God is calling them to do to help those in need in the most appropriate way. What Nehemiah did was to remind the people that God had given him responsibility for what was at stake and to remind them that God was with them. Sometimes, such encouragement

---

161   Matthew 18:19-20
162   Matthew 18:18 (The literal translation makes it plain that we are binding whatever has already been bound in heaven and loosing whatever has already been loosed in heaven. This changes the meaning of this verse, of course!)

is all that is needed to enable people to be able to continue the journey they are on. This was the case in the next part of the story:

> *From that day on half my men did the work, whilst the other half were equipped with spears, shields, bows and armour. The officers posted themselves behind all the people who were rebuilding the wall. Those who carried the materials did so with one hand and held a weapon in the other, and each of the builders wore his sword at his side as he worked. But the man with the trumpet stayed with me.*
>
> (Nehemiah 4:16-18; NIV)

The way these men stood together shows us how we are called to be there for one another, not only in prayer but also in practical ways too.[163] In fact, we should be willing to do for one another what Aaron and Hur did for Moses;[164] they stood with him until the battle was won, which is what we should be willing to do for each other through the storms of life.

Learning how to use the weapons given to us by God for the battles ahead is something better learnt from those who are experienced prayer warriors than from a message taught from the front of a meeting. This is because such messages can impart the principles involved, but they will not show us how to apply them in the different situations that we face. The best way to learn how to do so is by being with people who know how to use them effectively.

Supporting people practically while they are navigating a

---

163   Romans 13:8-10; Galatians 6:9-10
164   Exodus 17:8-13

storm can involve giving them things such as them the encouragement needed to keep them going in the way that Nehemiah did. It can also be driving them to an appointment or helping them out financially. To put it another way, it is about serving them in the most appropriate way,[165] because in doing so, we are serving Jesus.[166]

Of course, there is a community aspect to all of this, but before looking at that, let us go back to the story:

> *Then I said to the nobles, the officials, and the rest of the people, "The work is extensive and spread out, and we are widely separated from each other along the wall. Wherever you hear the sound of the trumpet join us there."*
>
> (Nehemiah 4:19-20; NIV)

We can see from this passage and others that Nehemiah prayed about and found practical solutions to the issues facing his community. We need to be prepared, not just to do the same kind of thing for our church communities, but also to be part of the solution too. Our commitment to God involves not only having a relationship with Him, but also playing our part in the life of His family too.[167] Although this is not always easy for us to do, doing so will bring its own rewards.

In Nehemiah 4:21-23 (NIV), we see something of the pattern for good leadership:

> *...we continued the work with half the men holding spears, from the first light of dawn. At that time, I also said to the people, "Let*

---

165 John 13:1-11
166 Matthew 25:31-46
167 1 John 5:1-2

every man and his helper stay inside Jerusalem at night, so that
they can serve as guards at night and workers in the day." Neither
I nor my brothers nor the guards with me took off our clothes; each
had his weapon, even when he went for water.

Nehemiah not only delegated the work needed to be done to rebuild his community but also played his part in doing what was required. Leaders who know how to serve their community in a practical way[168] and are willing to do so will be an essential part of rebuilding our church communities so that they can thrive. Also, having been part of several churches since I became a Christian in 1986, my experience tells me that servant leaders make for good churches just as healthy parents create good families.

Perhaps here, we need to remind ourselves that it is not just leaders who are called to have servant's hearts; it is all of us. This was, of course, the lifestyle Jesus modelled to His disciples in His life and ministry.[169] It is, therefore, something all of us are called to imitate as we do our part in fulfilling the Great Commission.[170]

---

168   Philippians 2:3-4
169   John 13:1-17; Philippians 2:5-11
170   Matthew 28:18-20

12

CARING FOR THOSE IN NEED

Now the men and their wives raised a great outcry against their fellow Jews. Some were saying, "We and our sons and daughters are numerous; in order for us to eat and stay alive, we must get grain." Others were saying, "We are mortgaging our field, our vineyards and our homes to get grain during the famine."
(Nehemiah 5:1-3; NIV)

I t is perhaps worth noting that the episode we are now going to look at happened when the community was facing external opposition. This is because when a community faces external opposition, it will inevitably expose the internal cracks that were previously 'papered over.' To put it another way, if a community is under pressure from outside, it will expose issues that may not have been fully evident before. This was certainly the case in Jerusalem in Nehemiah's day. We need to recognise that the pressures from our current situation will inevitably expose all sorts of underlying issues in our church communities, and we need to work on them, not just prayerfully, but with care as we return to having physical meetings once again for the sake of our long term well-being, either individually or corporately.

We can see that the situation of some members of the community in Jerusalem was extremely desperate because they were in the middle of a famine there. As can be seen from what is said, this was taking its toll on the families in question:

> *Still others were saying, "We have had to borrow money to pay the king's tax on our fields and vineyards. Although we are of the same flesh and blood as our fellow Jews and though our children are as good as theirs, yet we have to subject our sons and daughters to slavery."*

(Nehemiah 5:4-5A; NIV)

Some of the people living in Judah were in dire need of help and this will be the case in our church communities too. Moreover, the larger the community is, the greater the number of those who will need help of some kind, particularly if the church is in a deprived area. Having been in a church where roughly twenty per cent of the church had mental health problems of one kind or another, I know that sometimes the need can seem to be overwhelming. However, the first thing we need to do when we feel like that is to pray and ask God for wisdom in the way we deal with the people and situations in question, remembering that His heart is for those in need, especially those who are particularly vulnerable to mistreatment or abuse of some kind.[171].

---

171   Exodus 22:21-24

We may not always be able to meet every kind of need ourselves, either individually or as communities, but we do need to listen to what God has to say to us about the people and the situations we are made aware of unless there is an obvious solution to the problem.[172] Nehemiah knew instantly what the problem was and what needed to be done to put things right:

> *When I heard their outcry and heard these charges, I was very angry. I pondered them in my mind and then accused the nobles and officials. I told them, "You are charging your own people interest."*
>
> (Nehemiah 5:6-7A; NIV)

This may seem to be a strange thing for Nehemiah to have spoken to this group of people from a modern perspective, but that is because things are done differently in our culture and time. However, what Nehemiah was in fact saying to the community leaders was that they were breaking the Law, which states that no interest was to be charged for loans to fellow Jews.[173] This is partly why Nehemiah was so angry, although there were other reasons which will become more apparent further on in the story:

> *...I called together a large meeting to deal with them and said, "As far as is possible, we have brought back our fellow Jews who were sold to the Gentiles. Now you are selling your own people, only for them to be sold back to us!" They kept quiet, because they could find nothing to say.*
>
> (Nehemiah 6:7B-8; NIV)

---

172   Acts 6:1-6
173   Exodus 22:25-27

This verse provides two other reasons for Nehemiah's anger and clarifies the situation he is trying to deal with. Injustice of any kind should make us angry and fill us with a desire to see things put right,[174] even if we are not able to do anything other than pray into the situation in question. We will probably not see the kind of thing that Nehemiah had to deal with, but there will inevitably be situations in our church communities that are just as wrong, and we should not turn a blind eye to such things even if we want to.

In one of the churches I was a part of some years ago, I became aware of a situation involving an inappropriate relationship between one of the men in the congregation and a teenage girl a couple of months before it came to light. The problem was that I thought I was imagining it and did not say anything. I later found out I was not the only one who knew, but even now, I sometimes wonder whether if had I spoken up, maybe the outcome would have been different. Certainly, I would now be less reticent to speak out if I became aware of a similar situation, or for that matter, anything needing decisive action.

We cannot truly be the salt and light Jesus has called us to be outside of our church communities unless we are living like it inside them.[175] In other words, if we are not living the way God has called us to live, we will not be able to fully represent His Kingdom to those who do not yet know God in the way that we do. We will then fail to fully experience what God can do through us if we were doing so.

Nehemiah told the community leaders what they needed to do to put things right:

---

174   Micah 6:8
175   Matthew 5:13-16

I continued, "What you are doing is not right. Shouldn't you walk in the fear of our God to avoid the reproach of our Gentile enemies? I and my brothers and my men are also lending the people money and grain. But let us stop charging interest! Give back to them immediately their fields, vineyards, olive groves and houses, and also the interest you are charging them – one per cent of the money, grain, new wine and olive oil."

(Nehemiah 6:9-11; NIV)

We live in a day when truth is whatever you want it to be, and that means people think they can live in whatever way they feel is right. However, as Christians, we are called to live differently; to live in the light of God's word,[176] which is the plumb line of truth, and for His glory rather than our own. Nehemiah challenged the leaders of his people to do so by putting right the wrong which they had done to some of those under their authority and care.

We are called to not only forgive those who have hurt us, but also to seek to put right any damaged relationships whenever we can, including those where we were in the wrong. As we can see, what Nehemiah said to the community leaders was the beginning of the kind of process involved in doing so. Such a process involves more than an apology:

"We will give it back," they said, "And we will not demand anything more from them. We will do as you say." Then I summoned the priests and made the nobles and the officials take an oath to do what they said that they would.

(Nehemiah 6:12; NIV)

---

176   2 Timothy 3:16-17

The willingness of the community leaders to make restitution to those whose lives they had damaged is something we can learn much from. This is because while there is a lot of teaching about forgiveness today, there is not a great deal said about the process involved in restoring damaged relationships. This is probably because there is a cost involved and very few people are willing to challenge people to pay it. However, whatever the reasons are for this lack of teaching, the process involved would bring healing to those whose lives were directly affected by whatever happened and also restore unity to the body of believers they are part of,[177] so people are missing out on something of God's heart for them.

We need to also remind ourselves that God still wants to heal our wounds, [178]even if reconciliation is not possible for some reason. Forgiveness is the key to healing,[179] and therefore, it is the starting point for our wounds to be healed. Once we have worked through the issues involved, we can then ask God to heal the damage that was done.[180] If this is something that you are unable to do without external help, there are a number of good ministries that offer the kind of prayer being spoken of if it is unavailable in your local church.

After speaking about some prayers,[181] the story changes direction again:

Moreover, from the twentieth year of king Artaxerxes, when I was appointed to be their governor in the land of Judah, until his

---

177   Ephesians 4:3-4
178   Psalm 147:3
179   Matthew 18:21-35; Ephesians 4:32
180   Isaiah 53:4-6; 61:1-3
181   Nehemiah 6:13

thirty-second year - twelve years – neither I nor my brothers ate
the food allotted to the governor. But the earlier governors – those
preceding me – placed a heavy burden on the people and took forty
shekels of silver from them in addition to food and wine.

(Nehemiah 5:14-15a; NIV)

From this passage, we learn more about the character of
Nehemiah and that unlike his predecessors, he did not demand
his rights, nor did he take advantage of his position. We can
learn so much about good leadership and humility from him,
although our ultimate role model for both is Jesus.

While we are on the subject of good leadership and humility,
I would like to tell you a story about the leadership of one of
my previous churches that touched me profoundly, and it had
a lasting impact on me. However, I have to be careful how I
tell the story in question because I do not want them to be
embarrassed in any way, so I have changed the name of the
senior pastor involved in order to protect their identities.

One Sunday, our Pastor, David, knelt in front of the whole
congregation and asked our forgiveness for not having loved us
as he should have done. Having done that, he then went and
knelt in front of each of the other pastors and their wives before
symbolically wiping their feet with paper towels. When David
had finished doing that, all of them got up and started to do
the same thing for all those who were in the meeting. To begin
with, the room was quiet but gradually, people started quietly
sobbing and then the presence of God manifested powerfully
in the room. No one who was there that day was the same
afterwards. Not only that, the presence, power, and gifts of the
Holy Spirit were much more evident in our times together.

Going back to the story, Nehemiah goes on to comment that:

Their assistants also lorded it over the people. But out of reverence for God I did not act like that. Instead, I devoted myself to this work on the wall. All my men were assembled there for the work; we did not acquire any land.

(Nehemiah 5:15B-16; NIV)

This verse speaks of Nehemiah's attitude to his role as governor in the light of his faith in God. Such reverence for God speaks of the quality and depth of the relationship Nehemiah had with Him. What he said about the work is an indication of how he views his personal responsibility towards God and others—the connection he sees between the two. Personal responsibility is not something that is often spoken about these days, and yet, it is vital for each one of us to recognise what God expects of us in our lives with Him, as well as the connection between this and what we are responsible for with regard to our relationships with others.[182]

Nehemiah talked about the way in which he feeds over a hundred people from his table before asking God's favour for himself.[183] In doing so, some would suggest that he is rather being boastful in speaking about the people that he fed daily, but from what we have seen of Nehemiah so far, he was coming out of a place of humility.

---

182   1 John 4:19-5:5; 1 Corinthians 12:12-13; 21-26
183   Nehemiah 5:17-19 NIV

13

VICTORY AT LAST

When word came to Sanballat, Tobiah, Geshem the Arab and the rest of our enemies that I had rebuilt the wall and not a gap was left in it – although up to that time I had not set the doors in place in the gates – Sanballat and Geshem sent me this message: "Come, let us meet together in one of the villages on the plain of Ono."

(Nehemiah 6:1-2A; NIV)

Getting the wall finished was quite an achievement for Nehemiah, particularly in the light of the opposition they had already faced. The rebuilding of the walls had not been easy, but those involved had pushed through the barriers and achieved their objective, which exemplifies our journey into God's heart for us.[184] Our journey will not always be easy, but when we encounter difficulties, we can choose to use them as building blocks for our future or we can let them become barriers to entering our Promised Land.

Having heard the news about the wall, Sanballat and Geshem propose to Nehemiah that they should meet up, but he knew that they could not be trusted from previous encounters with them. Whilst Jesus told us to love our enemies,[185] we do need to be careful in our dealings with such people because, although an enemy can become a friend this will not always happen. Sometimes such people will always be hostile towards us as we will see as we continue the story that we are looking at:

But they were scheming to harm me; so I sent messengers to them with this reply: "I am carrying out a great work and cannot come down. Why should the work stop while I leave it and go down to you?" Four times they sent the same message, and each time I sent them the same answer.

(Nehemiah 6:2B-4; NIV)

Nehemiah knew exactly what Sanballat and Geshem's intentions towards him were, so he refused to grant their request for a meeting, using the work that he was doing as the reason. However, it is possible to misread people as things are not always what they seem to be, which is why Jesus told us not to judge one another.[186] We also need to be extremely careful in the way we use whatever we have been told about people because their motives in speaking to us in the first place could be questionable, to say the least. It is better to give people the benefit of the doubt than to rush in and perhaps say or do something that causes immense damage to them or their lives, or even worse, the lives of those around them.

---

185   Luke 6:27-29
186   Matthew 7:1-5

I know of a situation years ago where the interference of those around a particular couple nearly brought about the complete breakdown of their marriage. There had been some gossip in the church that the husband was having an affair. Somebody mentioned what they had heard to the wife, and since their marriage was already troubled, things just escalated from that point on. Somebody in leadership caught wind of what was going on. He intervened carefully and lovingly. His wise and godly counsel eventually resulted in the restoration of the marriage, but things could have ended very differently. What was said in this situation was not true, but even if it had been, the kind of approach taken would still not have been right. We need to pray before doing anything in situations such as this and ask God what we should do with what we know—if anything.

Our relationships are the most important part of our lives, and therefore, it should be our primary priority in life which means that we should invest in them, ensuring that our lives reflect that. One of the keys to developing good relationships lies in spending time praying about our relationship with the different people we are involved with, asking God to show us how He sees them and to enable us to love them in the way He wants us to.

Sanballat tries again, this time, by letter, to get Nehemiah to meet with him but was rebuffed:[187]

They were all trying to frighten us, thinking, "Their hands will get too weak for the work, and it will not be completed." But I prayed, "Now strengthen my hands."   (Nehemiah 6:8-9; NIV)

---

187   Nehemiah 6:5-8

Fear is one of the strategies that the enemy[188] uses to see if he can undermine our faith and prevent us from fully entering God's heart for us. The primary key to defeating his schemes lies in doing what James encourages us to do in James 4:7, which is surrendering to God. This is because in doing so, we are giving Him control of the situation. The Holy Spirit is then able to step in and help us.

However, we do need to be aware that the enemy will not give up and will go on attacking us in different ways, just as the people opposing Nehemiah did:

One day I went to the house of Shemaiah son of Delaiah, the son of Mehetabel, who was shut in at his home. He said, "Let us meet in the house of God, inside the Temple, and let us close the Temple doors, because men are coming to kill you."

(Nehemiah 6:10; NIV)

Here we see another attempt not just to frighten Nehemiah but to undermine him. Sadly, the enemy will try to use the people around us to discourage and defeat us, so we need to learn how to use not just the weapons that God has given us but also the armour.[189] Tom Marshall in *Authority in heaven, authority on earth*, describes exactly what that is in such a clear way:

The armour of God is a set of life condition that God wants to establish in you. And when these are established, they enable God to work and they prevent the enemy

---

188   2 Corinthian 2:10-11; 1 Peter 5:8-9
189   Ephesians 6:11-17

from working. ...As far as warfare is concerned the life conditions in Ephesians 6 are the critical ones. There are other important life conditions that are important to your maturity, growth and so on, but as far as defence is concerned Ephesians 6 names the critical ones.[190]

The life conditions given are:

- Truth (John 3:21)
- Righteousness (Romans 3:22-24)
- Peace (Philippians 4:7)
- Faith (Hebrew 11:1; 3:6), and
- Hope (Hebrews 6:17-20)

In other words, the armour is not something we can put on or take off as some people seem to suggest, but it is about our heart and how we live our lives. If we choose to live our lives in the way we want, even in what seems like relatively 'small ways' rather than living in the way God has called us to live, then we will not be able to enjoy the protection from the enemy which God wants us to have.

Let look at Nehemiah's response to Shemaiah and see what more we can learn from it:

But I said, "Should a man like me run away? Or should someone like me go into the Temple to save his life? I will not go!" I realised that God had not sent him, but he had prophesied against me because Tobiah and Sanballat had hired him. He had been

---

190   P171-172; Chapter 19 Authority in heaven, authority on earth Tom Marshall Sovereign World 2005

hired to intimidate me so that I would commit a sin by doing
this, and then they would give me a bad name to discredit me.

(Nehemiah 6:11; 11-13 NIV)

From this, we see that Nehemiah refused to be intimidated because he recognised what was said had not come from God. It can be rather difficult at times to recognise the source of what we are hearing, seeing, or experiencing. This is where the gift of discernment becomes essential,[191] as identifying the source of something is not an intellectual exercise but a spiritual one. In the past, people have often tied it to deliverance, but it is not limited to that, as it can be used to discern the source of a prophecy, a tongue, or teaching brought by someone. It is a gift that is much needed today and one we should all ask God for, particularly as we start rebuilding our lives and church communities.

Nehemiah's prayer shows us something of how he feels:

Remember Sanballat and Tobiah, my God, because of what they
have done. Remember also Noadiah and how she and the rest of
the prophets have been trying to intimidate me.

(Nehemiah 6:14; NIV)

Whilst this is not the kind of prayer we should be praying, we can still learn something from it, particularly about the prophetic, which is prone to abuse. This is largely caused by the lack of balanced teaching on it and the example set by a few who call themselves prophets but are not. In this verse, we see a prime example of someone who is misusing the prophetic for

---

191   1 Corinthians 12:4-11 note v10

personal gain, and the problem with such people is that they will always have apologists.

If someone gives a prophetic word that comes out of a wrong heart attitude, such as was the case in the quotation that we looked at earlier, or that is out of line with biblical truth that is generally relatively easy to spot. However, it is far more difficult to identify words that are coming from a wrong spirit and that is where the gift of discernment becomes crucial.

Having said that, it is important for us all to be aware that if someone has been well trained in the use of the prophetic (and the church/group that they are ministering in have a few simple guidelines to ensure that the gift is used properly) it can be life-changing not just for those who are given words, but for all who are present.

Finishing the wall within such a short period was an incredible achievement for Nehemiah and all those involved, but Nehemiah makes it plain to those reading his book that they could not have not done so without God's help:

> ...the wall was completed on the twenty-fifth of Elul, in fifty-two days. When all our enemies heard about this, all the surrounding nations were afraid and lost their self-confidence, because they realised that this work had been done with the help of our God.
>
> (Nehemiah 6:15-16; NIV)

Acknowledging that it is because of God that we are where we are is one of the hallmarks of the mature believer and will undoubtedly give us opportunities to speak about our faith to those who do not yet know Him.

What is particularly interesting about the quotation that we are looking at is the way in which the people of the nations around them attributed the speed at which the wall was finished to God. It raises the question of whether people see God in us as well as how our church communities are seen. Our witness is a vital part of our involvement in ensuring the ongoing growth of the Kingdom and it will not result in people wanting what we have if we are not reflecting Jesus in our lives in the way that we have been called to.

Even after the wall was finished, the opposition did not stop,[192] and sadly, the same will be true in our lives, although there will be seasons when it seems as if it has.

---

192   Nehemiah 6:16-19

14

CONSOLIDATING AND REVIEWING

After the wall had been rebuilt and I had set the doors in place,
the gate keepers, musicians and the Levites were appointed.
I put in charge of Jerusalem my brother Hanani, along with
Hananiah the commander of the citadel, because he was a man
of integrity and feared God more than most people do.
(Nehemiah 7:1-2; NIV)

Having completed the work on the wall and putting the gates in place, Nehemiah started delegating his authority by appointing people to look after the city (and the Temple) in various ways.[193] If you are someone who has authority over people, either inside the Church or out, you will know how difficult it can be to find the right people to delegate some of your authority and role to. Nehemiah's choice of people

---

is noteworthy particularly because of what he says about his choice of Hananiah. Integrity is not something that is spoken of or acknowledged as much as it once was yet as Christians it is something that we should want to have and be known for. However, it is not something that we can achieve in our strength as it flows out of our desire to please God and partnering with the Holy Spirit is a necessary part of the process needed for it to become a reality in our lives.

After he had sorted out the arrangements for the government and care of the people of Jerusalem, Nehemiah now started to look at other areas of life in the city:

Now the city was large and spacious, but there were few people living in it, and the houses had not yet been rebuilt. So my God put it into my hear to assemble the nobles, the officials and the common people for registration by families. I found the genealogical record of those who had been the first to return.

(Nehemiah 7:4-5A)

At this point in the story, Nehemiah started to review the situation to see what needed more to be done to finish the work of restoration he had embarked on. We need to do this at intervals in our lives to know whether we are at the right place. Such reviews can be a healthy exercise if done prayerfully and it is something we should do regularly as we rebuild not only our lives but also our church communities. Such assessments can lead to the identification of 'course changes' that we need to make so that we can enter fully into God's heart for us.

Having spoken about the records Nehemiah then goes on

to detail what he found out.[194] Such records were essential in the years prior to the sacking of the Temple as it was through them that someone whose Jewish heritage was uncertain would have been verified. This was the kind of evidence required to claim an inheritance amongst other things.

Returning to the story we now read that:

> *When the seventh month came and the Israelites had settled in their own towns, all the people came together as one in the square before the Water Gate. They told Ezra the teacher of the Law to bring out the book of the Law of Moses, which the Lord had commanded for Israel.*
>
> (Nehemiah 7:73B-8:1; NIV)

From what we have just read we can see that previous events in the lives of the people of Judah had awakened a hunger in their hearts for God hence their desire for Ezra to bring out the Law. Such hunger is the hallmark of the beginning of a revival and I can testify to the way in which it multiplies and grows from relatively insignificant beginnings. Having experienced two 'outpourings' of the Spirit, one when I lived in London and the other when I was living in the Nottingham area, I am speaking from first-hand experience. I have referred to them both as being outpourings because I am not sure that either them exhibited all the hallmarks of a full blown revival - although I know that some of the people who shared those experiences with me would probably disagree as there is no real consensus on what revival looks like!

Perhaps here, we need to remind ourselves that what is

---

194   Nehemiah 7:5b-73a

referred to as being the book of the Law of Moses is just the first five books of the Bible, sometimes referred to as the Pentateuch. In Ezra's day very few people would have been able to read and even less would have had access to the Law or even any understanding of it. We are incredibly privileged in this country now as the Bible is accessible to us all and in a variety of different ways. As such we should pay attention to it as the people of Judah did:

> ...on the first day of the seventh month Ezra the priest brought the Law before the assembly, which was made up of men and women and all who were able to understand. He read it aloud from daybreak till noon as he faced the square before the Water Gate in the presence of the men, women and others who could understand. And all the people listened attentively to the Book of the Law.
>
> (Nehemiah 8:2-3; NIV)

Looking at the above in the light of what appears to be a general lack of appetite for the Bible in this country, this is truly extraordinary and needs to be recognised as such. Our churches and our nations would be transformed if such a degree of hunger existed in our countries as was the case in Judah in Ezra's day!

The problem today is, many people do not want to live in the way God wants, and because of that, the truths of the Bible are challenged and questioned. In fact, for many people, truth is basically whatever you want it to be, whereas for us as Christians, our lives should be built on the principles of the Kingdom and the foundational truths God has given us in the Bible.

Teaching twelve-step programmes, books, etc., will only take us so far and will eventually limit our ability to become all that

God wants us to be, and this will hinder us from fully entering into all He wants to give us. Ultimately, our lives need to be built on the principles of the Kingdom,[195] and our trust needs be in the One who was and is the incarnate Word.[196]

Ezra then goes on to relate how things were done during their time together and who did what[197] before urging the people to:

"Go and enjoy choice food and sweet drinks, and send some to those who have nothing prepared. This day is holy to our Lord. Do not grieve, for the joy of the Lord is your strength." The Levites calmed all the people, saying, "Be still for this is a holy day. Do not grieve."

(Nehemiah 8:9-10; NIV)

Having heard the Law, the people knew just how far they had fallen short of God's standards, and their hearts were grieved, but Ezra encouraged them to recognise God's grace and His invitation to them before doing anything else. In other words, Ezra urged all those who were present to celebrate at that point what God had done and was doing in their midst, rather than grieving the failures of the past or the resulting losses. Celebrating at such a time was probably not easy for some of them, and yet, it is often in the place of gratitude God does His greatest work in our lives. This is because in such moments we are the most open to Him.

Celebrating the end of the lockdown or pandemic is something that all of us should perhaps consider doing individually and

---

195   2 Timothy 4:16-17
196   2 Timothy 4:16-1
197   7
Nehemiah 8:4-8

in our church communities. Doing so in whatever way seems to be the most appropriate, given our circumstances, could prove to be invaluable in reaching those who live or work around us with the gospel of the Kingdom.

> *On the second day of the month, the heads of all the families, along with the priests and Levites, gathered around Ezra the teacher of the law to give attention to the Law. They found written in the Law, which the Lord had commanded through Moses, that the Israelites were to live in temporary shelters during the festival of the seventh month...*
>
> (Nehemiah 8:13-14; NIV)

What is key in this part of the story is that for these people to be willing to gather again so soon after that meeting clearly shows us what their priority in life was. All of them were willing to drop everything or to put it into modern language, 'clear their diaries' to make room for God. This begs the question of whether we would be willing to do the same or if God is as important to us as we claim He is.

We have probably all heard the phrase that actions speak louder than words and what the people of Israel did now shows us even more clearly where their hearts were at:

> *...the people went out and brought back branches and built themselves temporary shelters on their own roofs, in their courtyards, in the courts of the house of God and in the square by the Water Gate and the one by the gate of Ephraim.*
>
> (Nehemiah 8:16; NIV)

What is amazing that these people did not just listen to the Law but responded to what they heard by wanting to live according to what was said. They saw what had been read as God's heart for them and their lives, not just something full of suggestions or ideas to think about. This begs another question, namely that of whether we have the same attitude to God's Word as they did. If not, why not? After all, in James 1:22-25, it speaks of doing what the Word says and the freedom it brings. So, not doing so is the equivalent to shooting ourselves in the foot!

The feast that was celebrated was the Feast of Tabernacles, which was discussed briefly earlier in this book. We, therefore, already know that it is not only connected to the Exodus, but its significance speaks of God being with us and of the rest of faith. However, what significance does it have at this point in the story of the people of Judah? What can we learn from it for our journey into God's heart for us?

For the people of Judah, this feast would have reminded them of how God fulfilled His promises to them in the past, especially the way He delivered them from Egypt and brought them into the Promised Land. That history with God would have undoubtedly reminded them of His promise at the time of exile to bring them back to the land [198] and would have also given them hope for the future. This should encourage us to entrust our future more fully to God because of His faithfulness to His people even in their times of disobedience.

Continuing on from where we finished we read that:

Day after day from the first day to the last Ezra read from the book of the Law of God. They celebrated the festival for seven days,

---

198   Deuteronomy 30:1-5

and on the eighth day in accordance with the regulations, there was an assembly. (Nehemiah 8:18; NIV)

What we see in the quotation just given is the way the people of Judah celebrated the feast and their desire to do things the way God wants them. There is also evidence of a change of direction for them as a people because they speak of changed hearts and lives. Perhaps we need to remind ourselves that our journey into God's heart for us involves our progressive transformation into the character and likeness of Christ,[199] and that repentance is an integral part of it.

---

199   2 Corinthians 3:18

15

REPOSITIONING AND REGROUPING

On the twenty-fourth day of the same month, the Israelites gathered together, fasting and wearing sackcloth and having dust on their heads. Those of Israelite descent had separated themselves from all foreigners. They stood in their places and confessed their sins and the wickedness of their fathers.

(Nehemiah 9:1-2; NIV)

O nly a matter of days after celebrating the Feast of Tabernacles, the people of Judah gathered again to make public their contrition over their sin. Hence, sackcloth and ashes. To do so, they separated themselves from all those who were not Jewish, thus setting themselves apart for God. For us, this is a picture of how God wants us to live; we are to be in the world but not be part of it.[200] In other words, we are called to live in such a way that we reflect something of the life of God that is in us.

---

200   1 John 2:15-17

The depth of commitment of the people of Judah to live for God rather than for themselves becomes even clearer in the next verse:

They stood where they were and read from the Book of the Law of the Lord for a quarter of the day, and spent another quarter in confession and in worshipping the Lord their God.

(Nehemiah 9:3; NIV)

They read the Law not only because it showed them how to do so, but also because it highlighted where they had failed to meet the mark. They also had a passion for His Word, and it is something we can learn a lot from as we need both to become truly mature in the things of God.

Also, they started their time of confession by acknowledging who God is and remembering what He had done for their ancestors, thus celebrating His goodness to them as a people.[201] Once they had done that, they started talking about how their ancestors had become progressively more and more rebellious, despite God's continuing faithfulness to them.[202] At a point, during their prayer, the many warnings that God gave them about the consequences of their disobedience to Him were acknowledged, likewise when it became a reality for them as a people.[203] It is then that the prayer becomes rather personal:

Now therefore, O our God, the great, mighty, and awesome God, who keeps his covenant of love, do not let all this hardship seem trifling in your eyes – the hardship that has come on us, on our kings and

---

201   Nehemiah 9:4-15
202   Nehemiah 9:16-29
203   Nehemiah 9:30-31

leaders, on our priests and prophets, on our ancestors and all your
people, from the days of the kings of Assyria until today.

(Nehemiah 9:32; NIV)

It is clear here that the people of Judah not only acknowledged
the sin of their ancestors but also recognised the ensuing consequences on their generation. This principle often referred
to as the sins of the fathers being visited on the children, is
spoken of in different sections of the Bible.[204] The idea of generational iniquity is something some Christians have issues
with. However, there is a clear evidence of it in our lives and
families—one example being the issue of addiction, which tends
to be generational in nature. Moreover, Isaiah 53:6 speaks of it
as something that Jesus died for, which means it can be dealt
with as we progressively appropriate the finished work of the
cross in our lives.

Let us imitate how the people of Judah spoke about the
goodness of God in their prayers if we are not already doing
so. The same thing is true of this prayer:

In all that has happened to us, you have remained righteous; you
have acted faithfully, while we acted wickedly. Our kings, our lead-
ers, our priests, and our ancestors did not follow your law; they did
not pay attention to your commands or the statutes you warned
them to keep.

(Nehemiah 9:33-34; NIV)

Having acknowledged the goodness of God, they speak of their
sin as a people, and how His warnings to them about their disobedience had gone unheeded again. Obedience to God is not

---

204   Numbers 14:18; Deuteronomy 5:9

something we often hear like we once did, and while we are not under the Law like the days of Nehemiah, it is still an essential part of our journey into God's heart for us. In fact, according to 1 John, that is the evidence of our love for Him. The key to understanding its appearance in practice is enshrined in what is often referred to as being the royal law of love.

One of the things which have helped me get through difficult times, including the present pandemic, is to remind myself of God's goodness to me—the things He has done for me, as well as His promises to me. Doing this has given me hope for the future, even during the darkest times of my life.

The rebelliousness of the people of Israel is spoken of three times during the prayer:

Even while they were in the kingdom, enjoying your great goodness to them in the spacious and fertile land you gave them, they did not serve you and turn from their evil ways. But see, we are slaves today, slaves in the land you gave our ancestors so that they could eat its fruit. And the other good things that it produces.

(Nehemiah 9:35; NIV)

Each time, they were handed over to their enemies and they cried out to God for help. On two of those occasions, God intervened fairly quickly but on the third, He allowed things reach the point where His people were in exile before doing so. However, while they were back in the land, their heart cry was still a need for further intervention from God.[205]

In order to understand the backstory, we need to remember that throughout the Old Testament, obedience and blessing,

---

205   Nehemiah 9:32-37

same with disobedience and cursing, are linked. If you are not sure of the reason for this, it is connected to the Mosaic covenant, and the explanation for it is given in Deuteronomy 28:1-45. For us as Christians, the situation is different because Jesus took the curse upon Himself[206] although we will need to appropriate what He did for us in the same way that we do with regard to forgiveness.

The consciousness the people of Judah have of their sin shows us that their repentance is not just superficial but comes from the core of who they are:

> *Because of our sins, its abundant harvest goes to the kings you have placed over us. They rule over our bodies and our cattle as they please. We are great distress. In view of all this, we are making a binding agreement, putting them into writing, and our leaders, our Levites and our priests are putting their seals to it.*
>
> (Nehemiah 9:37-38; NIV)

Such a depth of repentance will always bring with it a changed life and is the hallmark of a true believer's life. The desire of the people of Judah to live differently is demonstrated by the agreement spoken of in the verse. However, for believers of today, the evidence is shown in the way that we live our lives.[207]

The agreement starts with a list of signatories[208] which includes most of the people whose names have been mentioned already in Nehemiah. It seems likely that the point being made here is that everyone involved had the responsibility to accept for themselves the values which characterise the whole.

---

206   Galatians 3:10-14
207   Ephesians 4:21-32
208   Nehemiah 10:1-29

If we are to walk in agreement with one another at all in our church communities, there need to be certain core values we all share, but we live in an age where it seems too many people want to live their lives as they see fit. This has impacted Church life to such degree that some Christians are rejecting biblical values while others have such a low view of it, believing it has little or no influence in their thoughts. As we begin to rebuild our lives and church communities, it is essential to teach and discuss these core values and what they are, as we need a strong foundation on which to build.

Not every Christian or church community will share the same values nor should they be expected to, but a consensus on certain issues is needed. What those are may differ in some communities, and even within some of the groups that come under the same banner. However, our values as Christians or as communities must never be forced on others. They need to be given the room to be able to make their own choices and decisions. Should those who want to join our communities have different values to us, we need to give them time to either come into agreement with us or come to a place where they are willing to live in harmony with our values, even if they are not totally in agreement with them.

Looking now at the agreement[209] spoken of earlier, it is clear there are not many clauses in it. However, it is not as simple and straightforward as it looks. The key to understanding what is being said is that each clause is linked to the Law. In fact, each one of them has been written in such a way to give clarity and bring new understanding to certain aspects of it. Ezra had a good understanding of the law and reinterpreted it in such

---

209   Nehemiah 10:30-39

a way that others were able to understand it too. People like Ezra have a deep relationship with God, possess knowledge of His Word and the wisdom to apply it properly. All these things are of more worth than gold.

The agreement came about because the people of Judah wanted to do more than making a statement of good intentions which can easily and quickly be forgotten. They recognised that they needed something more concrete to mark and express their commitment to a complete change of lifestyle. For most of us, if not all, the lockdown should be a time of reflection and ignite a desire to live differently. Perhaps we too need to find a way to mark that decision? Not with a written agreement as it can easily be forgotten, but with something tangible which will act as a reminder of that commitment. I have various objects on my shelves that serve as reminders to me of such decisions over the years of my Christian life. The most recent one is a stone I dated and painted a specific picture on to remind me of what I did.

The resettling of Jerusalem is relatively straightforward and is given in the following verses:[210]

> *Now the leaders of the people settled in Jerusalem. The rest of the people cast lots to live in Jerusalem, the holy city while the remaining nine were to stay in their own towns. The people commended all who volunteered to live in Jerusalem.*
>
> (Nehemiah 11:1-2; NIV)

The gathering of our church communities again may not be as straightforward as we would like, and the reasons are best

---

210   Nehemiah 11:3-12:26

known to us. Some churches may have lost their buildings or no longer have access to the places they used to meet. Others may not be able to gather as they did before because of the issues created by social distancing. Moreover, we may find that some churches may have to offer the use of their buildings to other churches to enable them to meet. Not only that, but some may also be encouraged to volunteer not to attend meetings to allow others the opportunity to do so.

16

DEVELOPING AND MOVING ON

At the dedication of the wall of Jerusalem, the Levites were sought out from where they lived and were brought to Jerusalem to celebrate the dedication with songs of thanksgiving and with the music of cymbals, harps, and lyres. ...When the priests and the Levites had purified themselves ceremonially, they purified the people, the gates, and the wall.

(Nehemiah 12:27, 30; NIV)

There are three dedications mentioned in Ezra and Nehemiah, the two books we have been discussing. The first dedication was to do with the Temple,[211] the second was that of the people,[212] and the third is the dedication of the wall.[213] For us, these could be typifying the rededication of our lives to God, both individually and corporately, at different

---

211   Ezra 6:16-18
212   Nehemiah 9:38
213   Ezra 12:27-43

stages on our journey into God's will. Certainly, there are times when it is appropriate or necessary for us to do so.

Moreover, we see the first part of a description of what seems to have been rather a spectacular celebration full of music and fanfare. It is rather difficult for us to imagine anything that would be comparable to this celebration because the culture of Nehemiah's time is so different from ours. A royal wedding would probably be the closest match to the celebration in view and the level of significance. In Christian terms, a possible comparison could be made with the Make Way marches of the eighties and nineties in central London or with some of the larger open-air events such as Spring Harvest. However, there is not much in terms of spectacle associated with these events.

Thanksgiving is spoken of in this celebration. This is a reminder that it is a vital part of our worship, and there are always things we can give thanks for even when circumstances are difficult. Moreover, it is something that we are actively encouraged to do both in the Old Testament and the New.[214]

Going back to the story we now read that:

At that time men were appointed to be in charge of the storerooms for the contributions, first fruits and tithes. From the fields around the towns they were to bring into the storerooms the portions required by the Law for the priests and the Levites, for Judah was pleased with the ministering priests and Levites.

(Nehemiah 12:44; NIV)

One of the things that I have recognised over the years is the necessity to balance the practical with the spiritual. Otherwise,

---

214   Psalm 100:4-5; Philippians 4:6-7

we can be so practically minded that we are of no spiritual use. In the quotation that we are looking we see something of the balance that has just been spoken of in the way that provision was made for those serving in the Temple.[215]

As we rebuild our lives and church communities, we need to be aware of the need for this balance and take it into consideration. The same is true of work-life balance. The key will lie in ensuring our priorities for our lives, both individually and corporately, are firmly rooted in the practicalities of life and Kingdom principles. Doing this is quite challenging as it will mean recognising true faith is not about accepting what others may see as being the realities of life.[216]In fact it may mean believing that what seems to be impossible is possible because nothing is impossible with God.[217]

Continuing with the story, we now read:

On that day the book of Moses was read aloud in the hearing of the people and it was found that no Ammonites or Moabites should ever be admitted into the assembly of God, because they had not met the Israelites with food and water but had hired Balaam to call a curse down on them. (Our God, however, turned the curse into a blessing.) When the people heard this law, they excluded from Israel all who were of foreign descent.

(Nehemiah 13:1-3 NIV)

Our understanding of not only the principles of God's kingdom but also of his character and nature grows as we read His Word and the Holy Spirit reveals the truth within it to our hearts. In

---

215   Nehemiah 12:45-47
216   Hebrews 11:1-40
217   Luke 1:37

the quotation we are looking at we see an example of this. Whilst it is not relevant for us today as God no longer excludes the people groups mentioned from becoming part of His people[218] still has a lot to teach us about application of truth.

By this time, Nehemiah had finished his first term of office as governor, but about fifteen years later, he began his second term. However:

Before this Eliashib the priest had been put in charge of the store-rooms of our God. He was closely associated with Tobiah and had provided him with a large room formerly used to store the grain offerings and incense and temple articles, new wine and olive oil prescribed for the Levites, musicians and gatekeepers, as well as the contributions for the priests. (Nehemiah 13:4-5)

This was probably the first thing that Nehemiah had to deal with on his return to Jerusalem.[219] Having thrown Tobiah out and purified the room, Nehemiah then had to deal with the surrounding circumstances.[220] When things go wrong in our lives, trying to sort them out again can be a very much complicated process. Some situations are very intractable, and resolving them can consume years of our life, particularly if there are people involved who do not want to be reconciled to you or do not understand the issues involved. It is vital in such situations to remember the encouragement of James 1:2-4:

Consider it pure joy, my brothers and sisters, whenever you face trials of many kinds, because you know that the testing of your

---

218   Matthew 28:18-20; Galatians 3:28
219   Nehemiah 13:6-9
220   Nehemiah 13:10-14

faith produces perseverance. Let perseverance finish its work so that you may be mature and complete, not lacking anything.

You may have heard that it has been said that God is more interested in developing our character than our comfort. However, whilst there is truth in this statement, it is incomplete. Since God loves us unconditionally, His desire for us is to become the people He made us to be so that we can live fulfilled and rich lives.

What we have been going through is akin to what is referred to as the Blitz in some ways. That too involved the restriction of peoples' lives in a variety of ways and was likewise a traumatic event for all who lived through it just as our situation now is. The country passed through a major economic, sociological, and cultural change afterwards, as will undoubtedly be the case once this pandemic is over. This book has primarily been about navigating what is happening to us now in partnership with God. This is because as we walk through the situations of our lives with God, His work of transformation is done in our lives.

The work of transformation does not happen through just one means but through many, most of which have been spoken about or mentioned in this book. The key to unlocking that lies in our relationship with God whilst the key to understanding the different ways in which God works in our lives is in the Word of God. This is one of the reasons that we need to read it regularly.

The rest of the chapter focuses predominantly on issues surrounding the care of the Temple, caring for those whose lives are being spent in running it, and the purity of the community (Nehemiah 13:3:15-30). From this, we can see another hallmark of a good leader, which is being able to recognise when things are not right within the life of our church communities and being able to deal with them. In other words, ongoing maintenance is not just something we do on our cars or homes but is something that we need to do in our church communities and lives.

Throughout this book, we have looked at a variety of things we may need to deal with as we start rebuilding our lives and church communities—the primary one being prayer and working in partnership with the Holy Spirit. There is, however, one final thing I would like to address, and that is the need to think outside the box as we start to rebuild. If we try to go back to the kind of life we used to live, it will not work because whether we know it or not, what has happened to us has changed us. Therefore, we need to be more creative and dream a little with God as we now have the opportunity to change not only our lives but also our church communities.

Finding the new normal for us individually and corporately is not going to happen overnight. It is going to be a journey and our attitude to what has happened will largely decide whether it becomes one that is a constant struggle or one that we enjoy. For that to be the case, we will need to be there for each other, remembering that we are all part of God's family. We will particularly need to keep on encouraging one another in the Lord as we are urged to in 1 Thessalonians 5:11, otherwise we will quickly run out of steam. Here are some verses from one of the Psalms that I have found to be encouraging and I hope that you will too:

How enriched are they who find their strength in the Lord; Within their hearts are the highways of holiness! Even when their path winds through the dark valley of tears, they dig deep to find a pleasant pool where others find only pain. He gives to them a brook of blessing filled from the rain of an outpouring. They grow stronger with every step forward until they find all their strength in you, and the God of all Gods will appear before them in Zion. [221]

Let me finish by saying that I believe what we have gone through is preparation for whatever is going to happen now. We are at the end of what is often referred to as the end times and the time is drawing close for Jesus to return.[222] Could whatever is coming perhaps be the lead up to it? I am sure that most of us, if not all, are beginning to ask such questions. Whatever the case is, let us not be like the five foolish virgins[223] but let us be ready for what is coming...

---

221   Psalm 84:5-7 tPT
222   Matthew 24:36-44; Acts 1:11
223   Matthew 25:1-13

INDEX OF KEYWORDS/THEMES

ALSO BY JAN TAYLOR

A Community of Love
Jan Taylor

This book describes something of what the Bible tells us about the Church being God's family and how He sees it.

It covers topics such as the Priesthood of all believers, the Body of Christ, the door of worship, the house of prayer, washing one another's feet, the bond of peace, the structure of leadership, shepherding the flock, the value of vision and the importance of discipleship. It has been written for both those who have been Christians for a long time, as well as those who have recently found faith as it is designed to underpin whatever understanding those reading it have of the Church.

ISBN 978-1-911211-91-4

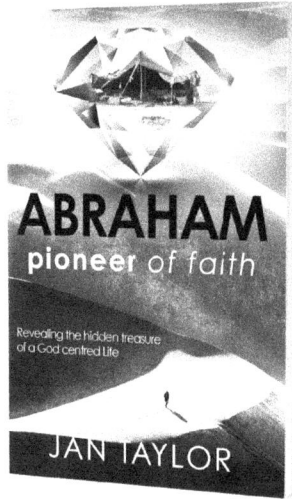

Abraham: Pioneer of Faith
Jan Taylor

This book is for Christian pilgrims that yearn to discover the treasures to be found deep within our relationship with God.

Delve into the spiritual principles behind the extraordinary journey of Abraham and see how they can be applied to our life today. As we seek to connect with God, Abraham's story is unpacked to help us progress our own journey of faith into God's heart – just as Abraham journeyed into God's heart for Him.

The author unpacks Abraham's faith issues and examines the call of God on his faith; his real failures and testing; God's covenant with him; his intercession before the Almighty. Vitally, you will see unfold in these pages the fulfilment of God's promises, which to him are looked upon as faith – it is when looking at Abraham's journey that we can truly understand what faith is and the hidden treasure of a God centred life becomes visible.

ISBN 978-1-911211-92-1

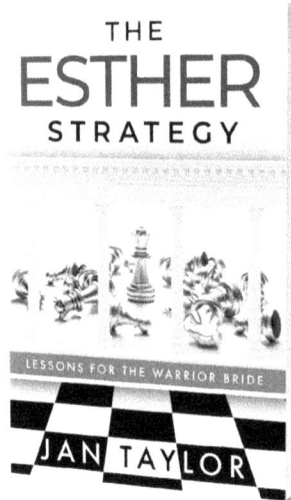

The Esther Strategy
Jan Taylor

This book is for those looking to understand how God can work amidst the most difficult of situations, offering biblical guidance for our own life struggles.

Do you have great obstacles in your life to overcome? Are you looking for proven biblical principles that take you from loss to victory? From the extraordinary story of Esther the author reveals a rich vein of life transforming principles aimed for each one of us. This book is no ordinary commentary on the story of Queen Esther but is rather a passionate revelation of what it means to walk in life-giving obedience to God's truth. With insights into the historical context, the reader is urged throughout to reflect on the parallels between Queen Esther's journey and our own. Taking Esther's heroic story and placing it in the heart of our own modern-day circumstances, this book will help give you a life strategy that is at the heart of God's purposes for you today.

ISBN 978-1-911211-93-8

CONTACT THE AUTHOR

JETthepilgrim@gmail.com

RECOMMENDED BOOKS

Authority in Heaven, Authority on Earth
Tom Marshall (Sovereign World 2005)

Celebrating Jesus in the Biblical Feasts
Dr R Booker (Destiny Image 2016)

Healing Victims of Accident and Trauma

Peter Horrobin (Sovereign World 2016)

The Bait of Satan
John Bevere (Creation House 1979)

The Sacred Journey
Brian and Candice Simmons (Broad Street 2015)

Unrelenting Prayer
Bob Sorge (Oasis House Network 2005)

Victory in the Wilderness
John Bevere (Messenger International 1992)

Lightning Source UK Ltd.
Milton Keynes UK
UKHW022025270721
387802UK00007B/433